The Econo...

The Economic Conundrum

Adam M. Tzagournis

Copyright © 2007 Adam M. Tzagournis
All rights reserved.

ISBN : 1-4196-2662-0
Library of Congress Control Number : 2006900869

To order additional copies, please contact us.
BookSurge, LLC
www.booksurge.com
1-866-308-6235
orders@booksurge.com

The Economic Conundrum

The views expressed herein are those of the author and do not represent the views of the broker-dealer for whom he is employed, its officers or its other employees.

TABLE OF CONTENTS

1. **The Nature & History of Money and Credit** 1

    What is Money? 1
    The Origin of Money 2
    Credit Before Coinage 4
    Coinage 7
    Coins & Inflation 7
    Gold-Backed Money 8
    The Changing Face of Money 9
    Fiat Money and John Law's Mississippi Bubble 10
    Money Supply and Credit Today 11
    Problems With The Current Fiat Money-Based System 14
    Inflation and the Consumer Price Index 19

2. **The Federal Reserve** 23

    The First Three Central Banks 23
    Reasons Cited for the Establishment of the Federal Reserve . 23
    The National Monetary Commission 24
    The Birth of the Federal Reserve System 26
    Fiat Money in America 27
    Advantages of a Gold Standard 28
    How the Federal Reserve creates money out of thin air 28
    The US Dollar Becomes Pure Fiat Money 31
    Bretton Woods and the Dollar Standard 31
    The Fed Goes Off the Gold Standard 32
    Paul Volker 33
    Alan Greenspan 35
    Bernanke's Helicopter Money to Fight Deflation 37

3. **The Role of Financial Intermediaries** 43

    Securitization 43
    Government Sponsored Entities (GSE) 44
    The History of the GSEs 45

    Favors Afforded the GSEs................................46
    Size Matters..49
    Company Risk..49
    OFHEO's Investigation 52
    Systemic Risk Posed By the GSEs......................... 55

4. A Leveraged System & Its Players 59

    Leverage 59
    Derivatives...60
    Various Types of Derivatives.............................. 61
    Risks and Rewards Associated with Derivatives 65
    Warnings from a Market Guru...........................70
    Hedge Funds 71
    Differences between Mutual Funds and Hedge Funds 73
    Regulation 73
    Hedge Fund Strategies....................................75
    The LTCM Story 77
    Systemic Risk..79

5. Debt and Deficits 83

    US Government Deficits 84
    US Government Indebtedness............................87
    Contingent Liabilities 88
    Private Investment.......................................93
    Consumer Spending......................................94
    The Trade Balance 95

6. The Dynamics of a Bubble............................ 103

    History of Bubbles 103
    Real Estate Bubble?.....................................109
    Signs of Froth in Housing 115
    Implications of a Bursting Housing Bubble
        on the US Economy 119

7. The Resolution of Economic Imbalances 123

    Vulnerabilities 126
    The Conundrum Explained 134

Dedicated to the members of my family for their patience and understanding, to the members of my team for their dedication and hard work, to my clients for constantly challenging me to be the best portfolio manager I can be, and to the good Lord for providing me with such a fulfilling and enjoyable occupation.

Chapter 1

The Nature & History of Money and Credit

Far too often, debate on economic matters ignores the basic principles that serve as the foundation of an economic system. This is indicative of either a lack of knowledge of those principles or a failure to understand how they interact. History is replete with lessons that we should closely examine. As with other disciplines, history serves as a wonderful laboratory that can be used to observe and study economic behavior. Rather than beginning a study of economic thought at some arbitrary midpoint, one must go back to the basics and gradually build from that foundation to better understand our complex system.

The essence of an economy consists of individuals' needs and wants, and the behavior they undertake to fulfill them. Nothing is more basic to economic function than the concepts of money and credit. These serve as the lifeblood of an economy acting to facilitate the transfer of our efforts into the acquisition of goods and services used to fulfill our desires.

What is Money?

Money is defined as a store of value and medium (or widely accepted commodity) of exchange for final payment – no other transactions are required. When standardized, money additionally serves to simplify financial calculations by providing a unit of measure. Credit is defined as an agreement in which a borrower receives something of value and agrees to repay the lender at a later time.

The noted economist of the Austrian School[1], Ludwig von Mises, described money simply as the 'most marketable commodity': "It is the most marketable good which people accept because they want to offer it in later acts of impersonal exchange."[2] Meaning that money has value because not only do people believe that they can use this money to purchase goods and services now, but if they so choose, they can save it and use it in the future because it will continue to have value.

So what is it that makes a commodity valuable and suitable to save in the first place? What makes it used and accepted universally? Throughout history – as society evolved – people preferred as a medium of exchange, those commodities that possessed certain traits. Such commodities were:

1. Valued universally
2. Easily divisible and valuable even in small quantities
3. Durable
4. Portable
5. Uncommon and costly to produce in order to maintain their rarity
6. Easily standardized, i.e., one unit equaled another in value

Money did not always exist in the forms in which we see it now, and it didn't always perform the functions it does today. History has taught us a great deal. The road that money – in all its various forms – has traveled through the years shows us what worked and what didn't. And when society chooses to ignore those lessons – and we are doing that right now – we face potential financial crises, similar to what Greece and Rome experienced in ancient times and Germany and Argentina in modern times.

The Origin of Money

In order to trace the evolution of money to the present day, consider what life was like before money existed and the circumstances in which money evolved into the many forms it appears in today. Up until around 4000 BC, in civilizations along the banks of the Tigris and Euphrates, people were able to do a variety of different jobs acceptably well. They grew or hunted their food, used animal skins to make their own clothes and were basically self-sufficient. What little they didn't have and yet needed, they could exchange for with others; their needs were simple and limited. It's what we all know as the basic barter economy. If you were short of grain but you'd caught a few fish that day, you could exchange the fish for some barley. You could further exchange the barley for some fruit. This was fine until the population grew and became more complex. Occupations began getting specialized: individuals moved into distinct lines of work like fishing, growing fruit, baking, mining, etc. It was around 3500 BC that the first cities with their temples and crowded streets were born. The new cities required specialist artisans: stonemasons, carpenters, weavers, silversmiths and others. And these artisans were neither self-sufficient, nor did they always have products with which to barter. That's when barter became more difficult.

If a carpenter needed some barley to last him a couple of weeks, he had to find a farmer in need of a wagon at that exact time. But a wagon was worth far more than a couple of weeks' ration of barley. So he needed to find a farmer who was not only in need of a wagon but one who also possessed three months' ration of barley and was willing to exchange that for a wagon. The odds began to stack up against the carpenter. It was the same for the stonemason who wanted to buy some fruit from a fruit farmer and was willing to pay for it, perhaps by building her a wall around her orchard. But what if the fruit farmer didn't need a wall? How was the stonemason supposed to pay for his fruit? Barter worked well when there was a mutual coincidence of requirements. When this coincidence didn't exist, trade hit a roadblock.

One simple way around the limitations of the barter system mentioned above was to find something that everyone wanted and everyone accepted as valuable, something that was easily available, a medium of exchange. The medium was commodity money. The value of commodity money derives from the commodity from which it is made. Gold, for example, is considered commodity money. Gold as a substance is valued for its characteristics, i.e. beauty, durability, malleability, etc. Alternatively, a modern-day dollar bill is not commodity money – the cost of producing a dollar bill is about 4 cents worth of ink and paper. Depending on location, availability and preference, various communities agreed upon different things to function as commodity money. Coastal communities valued cowrie shells, fishbone, whale teeth or fish oil, while farming communities used livestock, grain and farming tools as money.

As cities grew and trade between them flourished, certain kinds of commodity money used in some areas were not held in the same high esteem in other areas. The commodities for which people found a ready market became the most popular media of exchange which, in turn, further increased their acceptance and marketability compared to other media.

In Darwinian fashion, various forms of commodity money were

discarded for various reasons. Eventually, people began to prefer precious metals like gold and silver because of their convenience. Commodities like livestock, grain, oil, etc. were difficult to carry and vulnerable to spoilage, accidents and natural calamities. The portability of gold and silver made them especially useful when it came to larger transactions because they were less cumbersome to transport than tons of wheat, for example. Moreover, supplies of gold and silver remained fairly constant from year to year so their value remained stable, making them the perfect commodity with which to value other things over a long period of time. So gold and silver were cast in rings, coils and ingots, in different, standardized weights and used to make purchases and pay taxes.

As commodity money evolved, complex calculations became much easier to carry out. Officials could easily calculate increases in taxes in contrast to their earlier head-scratching ordeal while they tried to figure out how to collect 15% more from a taxpayer who had paid his dues in the form of one horse the year before. It also simplified the prior example of the transaction between the wagon manufacturer and the barley farmer. The wagon maker could sell his wagon to anyone in need of a wagon in exchange for gold. He could then use some of the gold to buy grain from anyone who was willing to sell it.

Credit Before Coinage

Before communities started using commodity money universally, they developed another important concept – that of **credit**. By all accounts, credit predates coined money. Returning briefly to the stonemason and the fruit farmer, an easier way out for the two was to work out an understanding by which the farmer would give the stonemason several pounds of apples in exchange for a certain amount of construction work when he required it. The same could apply to a farmer who wanted a cowshed built and would pay for it with wheat. Only, he didn't always have enough wheat and promised to pay for the work in installments, perhaps after the next harvest. This was the earliest and simplest form of credit. It didn't take long for it to catch on once people realized how useful and convenient it was.

Clay tablets

As productivity increased, so did the need to provide secure storage for the citizens' valuable output. Glyn Davies, author of *A History of Money from Ancient Times to the Present Day* noted that in ancient Mesopotamia and Egypt, royal palaces and temples served first as secure warehouses for grain and other commodities[3]. Later they served as 'banks' that issued receipts to the original depositors who left their grain there either for safe-keeping or as tax payments to their rulers. These receipts representing ownership for different lots of grain soon came to be used to clear debts or make payments for other goods and services.

Economist and author, L.R. Wray[4] also traces the origin of money to ancient Mesopotamia and Egypt where farmers' tax payments were standardized in foodgrains. "These grain standards formed the basis for all the early money of account units, such as the mina, shekel, lira and pound. Money...originated...as the unit of account in which...tax liabilities were measured."

Wray contends that as kingdoms grew, rulers outsourced tax collections to private farmers and debts were recorded on clay tablets that were either stored in temples to prevent tampering or sealed in case tablets that circulated. Debts could be repaid by submitting another such debt-tablet, the case of which was broken to verify the terms of the debt. According to Wray: "...taxes, debts and price lists existed for thousands of years before anyone had the bright idea of reducing transaction costs by creating money through stamping precious metals to coins. Markets operated on the basis of credits and debits and even the smallest sales to consumers took place on credit *(much like that between the stonemason and the apple farmer)* which could be carried on the books of the merchant for years before being cleared."[5]

In effect, these clay tablets functioned like promissory notes do in the modern financial system – tradable liabilities that could be settled in exchange for either goods or services when it was time to pay tax to the government. When the debt was paid, the tablets were broken. In fact, these clay tablets and grain banks continued to be the backbone of Egyptian finance even after the introduction of precious metals as a mode of payment.

Tally sticks

Similar to clay tablets, tally sticks functioned as transferable, negotiable, non-interest bearing instruments. They recorded details of a transaction as well as the parties involved and were used to pay taxes, and became the preferred mode of commerce between private parties. Tally sticks originated thousands of years ago and were used in different parts of the world. European trade and commerce was carried out through a system of tally sticks[6] for over 700 years until 1826. Tally sticks were split in two with the King (or the creditor) keeping the stock (the "stockholder") and the debtor keeping the stub. Both halves bore full records of the transaction and thus protected both parties from fraud or counterfeiting.

Tallies gained acceptance and were highly marketable – after all, they were legally accepted tender to pay taxes. Due to the fact the King was usually in need of funds, he sold his 'stocks' through the royal exchequer or merchant banks and a market in government debt flourished in England. The tally stick was also used as the primary instrument of commerce between private parties throughout the continent.

The remarkable thing about this system is that originally, tally stick debts often worked without currency, meaning that tally-based debts were contracted in goods and services but not in money. Interests were therefore discounted (like present-day bills of exchange) and charged in goods and services. Gold and silver were used to make settlements between various tally stick economies but not always to settle debts within an economy. Like clay tablets, tally sticks could not be created out of nothing. They had an individual debtor backing the specified value with a promise to pay in certain goods or services. Tally sticks were created by levying a tax on the citizens. Bear in mind that money-changing merchant banks could not issue debt they could only trade them.

The clay tablets of ancient Egypt and Mesopotamia and the tally sticks of medieval Europe functioned for centuries without major financial reforms, currency crises or hyperinflation because they were efficient and practically fraud-proof. When the tally stick was finally abolished, it had little to do with the belief that it was an antiquated system. In fact, the abolition of the tally system was put in motion to provide official backing to the abuse of royal power to tamper with the economy. In his book *War Cycles/Peace Cycles*[7], Richard Hoskins says that the formation of the Bank of England is what sounded the death knell of the tally stick economy. "The irritation of having usury-money and tally sticks circulating at the same time ended when Parliament abolished the use of tallies for taxes in 1783. Circulation of tallies continued in the back country of England until 1826."[8]

It was perhaps coincidence, but the abolition of the tally-stick economy and the ascent of fractional reserve banking happened around the same time. When the Bank of England started issuing paper notes in 1694, it became possible for the government to legally 'create' money (debt/credit) out of nothing. The important concepts of fractional reserve banking and the creation of money without any backing, along with the financial dangers they present to our financial system, will be discussed later.

Coinage

As gold and silver became the primary media of exchange in Mesopotamia, Egypt and other Mediterranean civilizations, this ability to pay for anything with a single commodity dramatically increased trade. People living in a region could more easily buy things brought from afar allowing them to further specialize in the production of goods and services in which they held a competitive advantage. This increased productivity, in turn led to greater trade, consumption, booming economies, and wealth creation.

The only thing that these gold and silver pieces lacked was a stamp of authentication: the pieces of gold and silver might not be of the weight or purity they claimed it to be. Mesopotamian rulers tried to bring some authenticity to the weights by branding their seals on the stone weights used in the scales to check the weights of pieces of gold and silver. Other wealthy individuals wrapped their gold into piles and attached clay tabs marked with a seal to authenticate the contents. This, of course, was not enough in the long run and around 600 BC, Lydia, a kingdom in present-day Turkey, impressed the royal seal directly onto small, round pieces of metal made from electrum: an alloy of gold and silver. These were believed to be the world's first coins and they became popular because they were minted in denominations as small as $1/15^{th}$ of a penny and could therefore be used by the poor as well as the wealthy. Shortly thereafter, Greece turned out its own line of coins, with faces of its gods and goddesses imprinted on its currency. In a few hundred years, Alexander the Great acquired large amounts of gold and silver when he conquered Persia and issued coins bearing his own image: the ultimate PR exercise in ancient times.

Coins & Inflation

A drawback of this new, convenient form of money was its vulnerability to misuse by those who controlled it. Glyn Davies points out that inflation surfaced as a problem within 100 years of the invention of coins. Sparta captured the Athenian silver mines in 407

BC at Laurion, causing a grave shortage of pure silver coins in Athens. So over the next two years, Athens issued bronze coins with only a thin plating of silver and decreed that they were worth as much as the pure coins. The shortage became even worse as the old pure silver coins began to disappear from circulation because people kept them and spent the new bronzed coins for their purchases. This provided an early example of what is known as Gresham's Law[9], that bad money drives out good. In his play produced in 405 BC, *The Frogs,* Aristophanes wrote, "The ancient coins are excellent… yet we make no use of them (by hoarding them) and prefer (to spend) those bad copper pieces quite recently issued and so wretchedly struck". Commerce was negatively impacted as those providing goods or services demanded more of the bronze coins to complete a transaction even though they were decreed to be worth the same as the pure silver coins. This translated into inflation as the same goods required more 'money' to be purchased. These bronze coins were finally demonetized in 393 BC.

Two centuries later, the Romans resorted to something similar. When the cost of the Second Punic War took its toll on the Roman economy, the government 'clipped' the silver and gold coins, debasing them. When the coins passed through the government's hands, they shaved off a bit of the silver or gold and melted down all those bits to create new coins to pay their troops. Later still, they issued lighter and smaller coins but decreed that they were worth the same as their older, heavier counterparts. People soon realized what was happening: as the supply of 'money' had increased, each coin was worth less, thereby reducing its purchasing power. Similar to the previous example with Athens, people selling goods and services required a greater quantity of the lower quality coins to complete their transactions, resulting in widespread inflation. Gradually the silver content in Roman coins was reduced to only 4%, causing hyperinflation and an eventual breakdown of the Roman banking system in about 270 AD. Subsequent attempts at financial reforms failed, leading to a prolonged decline in banking in Western Europe, not fully recovering until the Crusades 500 years later.

Gold-Backed Money

During the 1600s when both public and private banks multiplied throughout Europe, English goldsmiths dealing in coins also offered depository services using their safes to keep valuables. They also began to function as bankers by giving receipts for the gold deposits. These receipts were literally 'as good as gold' as the bearer could exchange them for gold from the goldsmith at any time. When Charles I seized the nation's mint, people flocked in droves to these goldsmiths to ensure their valuables remained in safe custody. When they found their savings secure, the rise of goldsmith-bankers and the use of fully securitized, gold-backed receipts issued by them, accelerated. The notes (receipts) became popular and were used as money throughout the country because they proved to be a far more convenient alternative to carrying or exchanging physical gold or silver. This was the advent of gold-backed money, which partially supplanted the circulation of actual gold coins, or commodity money.

Soon, goldsmiths realized that these gold receipts were convenient for borrowers too and this spurred the development and popularity of 'banknotes' in England. The dollar bills we carry in our wallets are banknotes, which are promissory notes of the Federal Reserve Bank payable to the bearer on demand and are used as cash. Indeed, by the end of the 17th century, coins in circulation formed less than half of the total money supply in Britain, which included banknotes, tallies, other bills, etc. And all this time, these notes remained 100% backed by either gold or silver. The banker promised to exchange the specified amount of gold for the gold receipt or banknote. The banknote, therefore, was a derivative of gold.

The Changing Face of Money

Slowly, the goldsmiths – and by extension, the banks – realized that as not all the bearer certificates in circulation would come back to them for exchange at the same time, they could issue more of these notes in the form of loans than the actual amount of gold they held. So they issued more of these 'unbacked' certificates to borrowers. The new certificates, like the original ones, still claimed to be convertible into gold, but there was not enough gold in the vault if everyone wanted to exchange their certificates at the same time. The proportion of gold held in reserve with respect to the outstanding receipts came to be known as the 'reserve ratio'.

Once the reserve ratio fell below 1:1 (ounces of gold held verses ounces of gold represented by gold certificates issued), banking became very profitable. In addition to earning storage fees for holding depositors' gold, the bankers were also charging interest (payable in gold) on 'false' certificates written up without the equivalent asset in the vault backing them. This was the beginning of Fractional Reserve Banking *(Also see Chapter 2)*.

On occasion a bank would get too aggressive, issuing too many certificates in relation to physical gold held, and when depositors found out, they would clamor for their gold, causing a 'bank run'. Since the aggressive bank did not have nearly enough gold to cover the demand, it would be forced to close resulting in many depositors losing their savings. US banks operate under a fractional reserve system, where only a fraction of deposits are held at any one time, the rest being loaned out. Prior to FDIC insurance, many US banks and their depositors suffered similar fates as a result of bank runs.

Fiat Money and John Law's Mississippi Bubble

Another dangerous monetary concept that was experimented with in ancient times and always resulted in disaster -fiat money- rose again in the early 1720s, and 200 years later, the whole world would rush to adopt it. Fiat money is money backed by nothing except executive decree that it is worth a particular amount. It made its first contemporary appearance thanks to a rather clever and colorful individual named John Law (1671-1729), who changed the face of banknotes – and the way their worth was perceived.

Born into a family of Scottish bankers, John Law was a gambler and a convicted murderer, but nonetheless he was considered to be brilliant in matters of finance. Following his conviction, he fled to France where he renewed his friendship with the Duke of Orleans, the new Regent. The excesses of King Louis XIV left France's economy in a terrible state. The Duke turned to the Scotsman for help, and Law convinced him to establish the Banque Generale, a private bank with the ability to issue paper currency. Although some of the bank's shares were bought by the public, most of its capital was furnished by the government. Law believed that paper currency would stimulate its circulation helping to revive the economy. The bank's assets in gold and silver could back the paper, making it accepted as legal tender.

Law was also given control of the Mississippi Company to which the French government granted a trade monopoly in North America and the West Indies. The company sold stock and low interest government-backed bonds to raise money. Through clever marketing, investors enthusiastically bought the shares to participate in the company's business in the promising new colonies.

Later, the Banque Generale became the Banque Royale, resulting in its notes being backed by the government[10]. The new entity issued its own stock and bonds, purchased all of the outstanding government debt, and through a series of changes eliminated the gold and silver backing of its notes. The notes became 'fiat money', but were still backed by the government. For a while, growth was spectacular. The company soon controlled most of the French trade outside of Europe. More shares were issued and purchased by the French population, even its poorer citizens. In January 1719, shares valued at 500 livres rose to a staggering 10,000 livres by the end of the year, creating wealth for investors throughout France.

As France continued to print unbacked currency, the increased supply diminished its value, which was reflected by the rising prices of goods and services. In other words, it took more depreciated livre to buy the same goods and services, making the prices higher. Then Gresham's Law took effect: gold and silver were hoarded by the population and paper money spent. When the Mississippi Company's earnings did not meet expectations, panic occurred. Investors sold shares, tried unsuccessfully to demand gold in exchange for their notes, and watched inflation reach 23% in the month of January 1720. As expected, both the banknotes and the company's shares declined in value and Law lost control of the company. The Mississippi Bubble burst and France plunged into a deep economic depression. Law died penniless in Venice a few years later. France abandoned paper money for the next 80 years until banknotes that were fully backed by gold were reintroduced.

Money Supply and Credit Today

Today, despite the problems encountered by others throughout history, all economies in the world operate with fiat money systems; money's value is established by government decree, there is nothing tangible backing it. The nation's money supply is the total amount of money available in the economy that can be used to buy goods, services, securities, etc. The United States central bank, the Federal Reserve, gives a detailed report on the money supply on a weekly basis. The total amount of currency (cash and coins) in circulation makes up the money base, referred to as M0. However, people also hold money in various types of bank accounts and other financial accounts. There is an important distinction between money and credit that can be noted in the money supply measures. The following definitions apply to the various money supply categories:

M1: All currency (M0) plus the money in checking or demand deposit accounts: basically, money that is used to make payments.

M2: M1 + the amount in savings accounts, non-institutional money market accounts and certificate of deposit (CD) accounts not exceeding $100,000. This is money that can be easily and quickly converted into cash.

M3: M2 + CDs exceeding $100,000, institutional money market funds, repurchase agreements and Eurodollar deposits.

Oddly, the Federal Reserve decided to stop issuing M3 money supply figures after March of 2006. At that time, M0 stood at $734 billion, M1 was at $1.4 trillion, M2 at $6.8 trillion and M3 at $10.4 trillion. Remember the earlier definition of money as a medium of exchange, or a widely accepted commodity used to exchange as final payment for something. If one closely examines the components of money supply and assumes fiat money is true money, then true money is really only the currency outstanding and demand deposits, or checking account money (M1). Some would argue that savings accounts at a bank should also be included, but technically they are credit instruments made between a depositor (lender) and a bank (debtor), and backed by the Federal Deposit Insurance Corporation (FDIC), which insures bank deposits of up to $100,000 per account. CDs, money market funds, repurchase agreements and Eurodollar deposits are, in the true sense, credit instruments.

Economists and policymakers, when analyzing certain variables to predict economic behavior, rightly consider the availability of funds. The matter becomes more clouded when the economist must decide which numbers to analyze. Should he consider true money stock only? Should he consider the credit instruments included in M2 or M3? If corporations decide to refinance short-term commercial paper with longer-term debt, should the resulting drop in the money supply figures be analyzed as a reduction in available liquidity? If the economist is going to include some credit instruments that have money characteristics, should he be including certain others such as asset-backed or mortgage-backed securities that are not included in the money supply figures, yet represent massive dollars? These questions are much more than theoretical debate and semantics. Availability and perception of liquidity are strong determinates of investor and consumer behavior.

Perhaps we should even consider the appreciation of a home or stock portfolio as 'money'. There has been a proliferation of credit availability in the form of credit cards and lines of credit against homes along with other easy-term consumer financing. It is quite possible that a certain consumer will view the drawing on a home equity line of credit just as if he were making the purchase with a check from his checking account. He may further believe that the underlying asset or home will retain its increase in value, meaning he is merely spending his new-found wealth as if he found the money on a sidewalk.

Certainly, the end result of using credit to make purchases will ultimately have a dampening effect on future spending when it needs to be paid back. But in the present, if the consumer is not looking at it that way, his current behavior of spending his new-found wealth may be the same as if he actually possessed unencumbered money. Liquidity conditions in an economy encompass money supply as well as the ease and cost of credit. The important question when evaluating the potential of economic growth and price inflation is – what are the **liquidity conditions in the economy? One can state unequivocally that,** at least through 2006, liquidity in the economy could be considered bountiful.

Doug Noland, financial markets strategist at David Tice & Associates, discusses 'contemporary money' and its effect on the economy as follows[11]:

> "The vast majority of contemporary 'money' is comprised of electronic journal entries (debits and credits). ...Banks are only one of myriad institutions that issue monetary liabilities, and reserve requirements are today virtually irrelevant to the process of issuing new 'money'. A diverse group of financial institutions, including banks, GSEs, savings and loans, insurance companies, brokerages, money market funds, finance companies, 'captive' finance units (i.e. GE, GMAC) and Wall Street structured entities (special-purpose vehicles, CDOs, MBS, ABS), are all tightly linked through the money and capital markets. These institutions issue new liabilities to each other and expand assets (increase holdings of other's liabilities), creating marketplace 'liquidity' throughout the expansion process. Funds are created and 'transferred' among

various types of institutions through adjusting journal entries (debiting and crediting accounts), and there is today absolutely nothing special about bank 'money'. Many types of financial 'intermediaries' debit and credit accounts using the same processes as banks.

But having said all of that, the M's are only one facet of monetary analysis. The examination and analysis of credit are actually far more important. Traditionally, money supply (bank deposits) expanded right along with bank lending (the commanding source of credit growth). The Fed could manage credit expansion through adjusting bank reserve positions, and bank deposit expansion was a good proxy for credit growth. Generally, the monetary aggregates still expand as credit expands. But there are episodes where significant credit growth is accomplished through the expansion of non-monetary liabilities (longer-term, riskier debt instruments).

"..... Are new financial claims backed by productive investment; is new lending financing asset inflation or financial speculation? Analysts of boom sustainability, along with financial and economic fragility, want to know! And just as we must look to broad money as an indicator of the degree of credit expansion, we must think broadly when it comes to inflation as well. Inflation is a credit phenomenon with myriad and divergent manifestations."

Problems With The Current Fiat Money-Based System

When the French economy fell on hard times, John Law insisted that the French people accept unbacked paper money to be worth as much as the gold they wanted. He was trying to get people to believe that the paper money they held was actually worth just as much as the gold that used to back it. Nobody was willing to buy into that in 1721. Today, however, the situation is similar with fiat money but the world still has faith in the monetary system.

In his discussion on fiat money, Mises explains that when creating fiat money, the state abolishes existing contractual obligations, including its citizens' legal right to full convertibility of paper money into gold or silver. The state decrees that everybody accept such notes as legal tender even though it is not backed (fully or in part) by any tangible assets. Throughout history, fiat money systems have been rare and usually short-lived because of the inherent dangers. Fiat money systems have been born of excessive public debt: whenever governments have been unable to repay these debts in gold/silver, they have preferred to remove the physical backing instead of making the hard unpopular choices associated with debt reduction. The creation of fiat money is what happened in France during the Mississippi bubble and it happened in the US in 1971.

In the late 1960s and early 1970s, like John Law's over-issued banknotes, the US was printing too many dollars and living beyond its means. Foreign nations led by France demanded that the US exchange its gold for their dollar holdings as promised. The US was unable to withstand the drain on its gold reserves, prompting then president Richard Nixon to do away with the international gold standard for the US dollar converting it into a pure fiat currency. *(Also see chapter 2)* Following the abolition of the international gold standard, the price of gold shot up and climbed more than tenfold in just a decade- a clear indication that there were just far too many dollars being printed and spent in relation to gold.

Since the abolition of the gold standard, the world has accepted the dollar in its place, holding it in reserve as a de facto standard. In effect, money created by the Federal Reserve is spent overseas to buy foreign-made goods. Surplus dollars are bought by the central banks of China, Japan and other nations who then lend those dollars back to the US by buying our government bonds. Other nations' central banks recycle those funds back to the US, by buying our securities, in part to keep the value of the dollar higher, thereby keeping their goods competitively priced. Unfortunately, this cycle has turned the US into the world's greatest debtor nation, which we will discuss later.

Whether it was the Athenians in 400 BC or the Romans in 100 AD who debased their currencies, the Chinese in the 10th century after a failed experiment with unbacked currency, the Spaniards in the 16th century who financed their wars with debt and ended up bankrupt, or John Law's ambitious plan in the 18th century that ruined the French economy, a common theme emerges. When a nation manipulates its currency, economic participants (consumers, investors, industry and government) change their behavior, which serves to test the financial system. As long as economic participants in aggregate have confidence in the system, and the participants behave approximately as they would in a system where the currency is backed, the economy can appear normal for long periods of time.

However, when participants lose confidence in a fiat system, Gresham's Law takes hold. People will make decisions to convert their fiat money into things that have value, like spending it on real goods and services, or investing it in precious metals and other commodities. This activity manifests itself as price inflation. When an individual comes to believe that the currency he holds will be worth less later than it is today, he will be more willing to spend the money on goods that will require more of a depreciated currency to purchase later. He will also be willing to accept more debt since he can pay it back later using depreciated currency. Alternatively, he will not be willing to lend money to others since he will be paid back later with depreciated currency. These actions result in higher interest rates to compensate for the diminished purchasing power of the future payments. This inflationary scenario has significant implications for how investors and consumers should behave in order to preserve purchasing power.

The United States, after its independence, stayed on a gold standard for 75 years and the founding fathers unanimously agreed upon the limited issuance of money. Thomas Jefferson said that banking institutions were a greater danger to American liberty than any foreign army. He warned: "If the American people ever allow private banks to control the issue of currency, first by inflation, then by deflation, the banks and corporations that will grow up around them will deprive the people of all property until their children will wake up homeless on the continent their fathers conquered." In fact, Section 10 of the US Constitution provisionally forbade the government from making anything but gold and silver as legal tender stating, "No state shall...make anything but gold and silver coin a tender in payments of debt." When the Civil War began, the US went off the gold standard for the first time in order to increase needed financing for the war effort, promising to reestablish the standard once the war was over, which it did.

In Europe, World War I created one of the most staggering cases of hyperinflation in the wake of the huge war indemnity that the Allies imposed on Germany. The political uncertainty in Germany – especially after a failed coup attempt – led to a labor strike, falling production and rising prices. The government – short on gold reserves and under pressure by the allies to pay war reparations – went off the gold standard and printed vast quantities of unbacked money, which in turn led to a further rise in prices, a classic example of the insidious nature of inflation. In order for fiat money to maintain purchasing power, not only must its supply be constrained, but people must accept it with confidence as a medium of exchange; once they start to lose that faith, its value will decline. And this is exactly what happened in Germany.

Germany's hyperinflation reached extreme levels when prices rose every few hours and people rushed out to spend their daily earnings, knowing that the spiraling inflation would almost eliminate the purchasing power of their money by week's end. At times, paper currency was used to fire stoves because it was worth less than the wood or coal it could buy. Banks issued currency notes with a value of up to 50 million marks. In the end, this vicious cycle of hyperinflation was finally stopped by the government's decision to drastically reduce the money supply. The first attempt at doing this was the issuance of the Rentenmarch – with real backing of property to replace the old, worthless, Reich mark in- 1923. The following year, a gold-backed Reich mark was re-introduced and stayed as the German currency until the introduction of the Deutschemark in 1948.

Indeed, this kind of inflationary trend prompted countries to introduce new hard currency money: asset-based currencies. These asset-backed currencies combined aspects of both fiat and commodity-backed money. While it involved fractional reserve banking, there were limits to how much money could be circulated. And yet, governments failed to implement the right checks and balances, which led to further distress resulting in another failed experiment with money.

One such example is the recent Argentinean crisis. The country's condition prior to the crisis of the late 1990s was similar in some respects to that of the present-day United States. Without the financial discipline imposed by a gold standard, the government in a bid to lift the economy out of the hyperinflation of the late 1980s, set up a currency board and pegged its overvalued peso to the US dollar. Rather than being an unbacked fiat currency, the peso would be backed by an asset, the unbacked fiat US dollar. The peso strengthed for a while under this structure.

The strength in the peso emboldened the government to spend and public debt grew rapidly. At the same time, the artificially high peso harmed the export sector and resulted in rising unemployment. Capital flight occurred as investors and lenders converted their pesos into dollars and withdrew capital from the country. Severe inflation followed as confidence in the peso began to fade, prompting further flight of capital and creating a severe economic contraction. By 2001, there was uncertainty about the burgeoning public debt and whether the country would be able to make good on dollar liabilities that were backed by government debt and peso assets. This led to panic and $2.5 billion was withdrawn from the banks in a single day before the government imposed restrictions on cash withdrawals. With the banking system in collapse, the country had no choice but to go off the dollar peg as inflation hit 72% the following year. While there have been many causes ascribed to the Argentinean crisis, most economists believe it was the direct result of the government's inability to reduce its skyrocketing external and public debt. This made the economy and currency vulnerable to shifts in market perception. The economic conclusion was the government simply could not earn enough to service its external debt and maintain the peso's peg to the dollar.

The inherent nature of fiat money makes it vulnerable to abuse. Governments are free to print money, ostensibly to control liquidity, stabilize price movements and smooth out economic cycles. Instead, monetary decisions often create distortions in the economy. Whenever we allow such important decisions to be made by central bankers rather than the free market, we subject the economy to the imperfections associated with any other centralized group of decision makers. However honest, intelligent and experienced the board members might be, they are not infallible.

The central bank has been successful in preventing or minimizing economic downturns by providing abundant and inexpensive liquidity but this has both financial and economic implications that must be considered. One of the financial drawbacks to this strategy is that consumers and government have taken on enormous levels of debt that need to be paid back eventually. Excess liquidity and the absence of recessionary troughs for abnormally long periods of time, create distortions throughout the economy. Economic cycles of growth and recession are as natural as breathing. When an economy is allowed to 'exhale' (i.e., experience recession), the consumer realm will defer purchases, instead using the money to reduce debt and build savings. Within the industrial realm, recessions promote the elimination of bad investments and lead to the elimination of inefficient competitors. Recessions allow the stronger and more efficient industry participants to become even more efficient and better able to compete in a global economy. These are basic tenets in a capitalistic free market economy.

Inflation and the Consumer Price Index

Inflation is a monetary phenomenon – it is the increase in money supply that will often result in too much money chasing too few goods and services, causing a consequent rise in prices and a reduction of the currency's value. Inflation, in the classical sense is not, as many schools of thought insist, a general rise in the prices of goods and services; that is specifically known as 'price inflation'. This rise in prices is a consequence of increased money supply that has eroded the purchasing power of that very same money. Real incomes fall because it causes a drop in the actual value of the monetary unit, which undermines the production of real wealth.

There has been a 35-fold increase in M3 money supply since the Fed started keeping records in 1959, through 2005. Therefore, it should not come as a surprise that a dollar saved in 1913 (when the Federal Reserve was formed, ostensibly to 'manage' money supply in the country) is only worth 3 cents today. This means the dollar has lost 97% of its value in less than a century.

The consumer price index or CPI is the most common way to gauge price inflation. It is a basket index (valued as per a weighted average) of 364 items that supposedly represent the goods and services that the average American family purchases every month, including food, energy, tobacco, rent, consumer goods, etc. In recent years there have been a variety of changes in the way CPI is measured. Many of these adjustments occurred following the 1996 Boskin Commission Report, which suggested that CPI was overstating the cost of living by approximately 1.3% per year. However, in many ways the measure of CPI now underestimates the true inflationary picture.

There are several problems with the way CPI is measured. The term 'hedonics' is used to describe the added pleasure a consumer derives from the quality enhancement of a product change. When calculating the CPI, the Bureau of Labor Statistics attempts to measure the quality changes to products. For instance, if a product such as a refrigerator cools its contents quicker, but costs more, an adjustment can be made whereby the increase in price is eliminated for CPI purposes. Technology has increased the quality and functionality of many products like computers, TVs and automobiles, which appear as price decreases in CPI. However, the utility of a product is a personal assessment. A bureau employee cannot accurately assign a value to a consumer's perception of a product's quality improvement. A consumer may not care if an automatic seat warmer becomes standard in a new car, particularly if he lives in the south, but the CPI value of the car may be adjusted lower to account for the now standard item.

Product substitution adjustments can also alter the reported CPI. If the price of beef increases greatly, the Bureau may rightfully conclude that consumers will substitute chicken purchases for beef purchases, so the CPI will reflect chicken rather than beef prices. Furthermore, if the price of chicken jumps, pork may be used as a substitute. Perhaps if pork prices also increase, we could use rabbit meat as a substitute. Product substitution adjustments do a better job of assessing the cost of survival than the cost of living.

The CPI allots a significant 40% odd share to 'shelter'; however, it doesn't take into account the inflation in the prices of both old and new houses from 2000-2005. That's because starting in 1999, the index stopped tracking the increase in housing prices. Instead, it takes into account something called Owners' Equivalent Rent (OER), which is the rental value of an owner-occupied house. From 1999 to 2005, rentals rose far slower than actual property prices masking inflation's effect on CPI. According to a September 2005 release by the Office of Federal Housing Enterprise Oversight (OFHEO), the average home prices in America went up by 13.43% from the second quarter of 2004 through the second quarter of 2005. It was declared the largest increase in the past 25 years. And yet, figures released by the Department of Labor indicated only a modest 2.7% increase in the housing component of the CPI in the same period. The new method of measuring the increase in the cost of 'shelter' in the CPI has little connection with actual housing inflation, at least for this period, and therefore grossly understated the actual increase in the residential real estate market.

Another factor masking monetary inflation is the impact that imports from China and India have on the prices of goods and services. Although foreign competition results in a real benefit of lower consumer prices, it is dangerous for policymakers to focus on its effect on CPI and assume that all is well with monetary and fiscal policy. The monetary inflation may initially manifest itself in other areas such as financial assets and real estate not picked up in the CPI.

Recently, many investors have diverted an increasing amount of money into speculative ventures in financial and real estate assets, much of it borrowed against soaring home prices. In effect, the fairly stable CPI touted by the government as an all-is-well banner, has played a crucial role in inflating the credit bubble. Today's inflation is not a case of too much money chasing too few goods. Instead, it is about too much money chasing financial assets and real estate. Eventually, monetary inflation tends to be reflected in price inflation, even in the flawed CPI.

Monetary inflation has a way of creeping up on an economy, undetected. The longer it stays unrecognized and unaddressed, the more distortions it creates. When it is finally recognized and addressed it is much more difficult to return to an orderly condition.

Chapter 2

The Federal Reserve

The First Three Central Banks

The Federal Reserve was established in 1913 through an act of Congress but is not our first central bank. The country's first central bank, the Bank of North America, was chartered by the Continental Congress in 1782 and was modeled after the Bank of England. The bank only lasted one year and was then followed by the First Bank of the United States, which lasted from 1791 to 1811, and the Second Bank of the United States, which lasted from 1816 to 1836. These central banks, like the goldsmiths mentioned earlier, operated on a fractional reserve basis (only a fraction of total deposits were held in reserve), allowing central planners the flexibility to inflate money and credit. Political meddling, corruption and misjudgments led the central banks to inflate money and credit to the extent that great harm was done to the economies during those periods. In each case, increased money and credit led to price or asset inflation and a falling dollar, followed by an economic downturn.

Andrew Jackson described the Second Bank of the United States as "a concentration of power in the hands of a few men irresponsible to the people," and was elected President of the United States on a sound money plank. Jackson then fought to ensure that the central bank's charter which was expiring in 1836 was not renewed.

Reasons Cited for the Establishment of the Federal Reserve

The National Banking Acts of 1863-64 laid down norms for making and administering loans, but there was no single central bank at this point and therefore, no centrally managed system of controlling the nation's supply of money and credit. Under this system, each bank's money supply was directly linked to the value of the Treasury securities and gold it held in reserve. When Treasury bond prices fell, banks had to borrow money from other banks or restrict the amount of money they circulated through lending.

In the absence of a central bank, money supply was inelastic. Greater demand for money was met with higher interest rates for loans rather than an increase in the money supply itself, which would have been accomplished through central bank activity. When money supply was limited, a free market determined interest rates based on the balance between the demand for loans and the supply of savings. But, this system is also prone to boom and bust cycles even though inflation tends to be less frequent and severe and the currency is more stable. In the absence of a central bank, neither too high a demand for credit nor too low a supply of savings is counteracted with an infusion of credit from the central bank. This could lead to a credit crunch and an economic downturn. Recoveries from these downturns, however, do not have the added burden of unwinding the distortions ravaging inflation can impart on an economy.

The financial panic of 1907, created in large part from a credit crunch, jumpstarted the movement for the formation of what evolved into the Federal Reserve. Though centered in New York, the panic of 1907 had countrywide repercussions, leading to the collapse of several banks and businesses. It was perhaps also the first time that a private individual – J.P. Morgan, the founder of the biggest banking and financial firm in the US – poured funds into the banking system, acting as a de facto central bank, to help create liquidity and limit the economic downturn. This action undoubtedly contributed to moving public opinion in favor of a central bank to regulate banking and currency in order to avoid such panics.

The National Monetary Commission

Congress created the National Monetary Commission in 1908 to study and make recommendations regarding the regulation of banking and currency. The Commission was headed by Senator Nelson Aldrich (R-RI) who, in January 1911, proposed the Aldrich Plan to Congress. It envisaged the creation of a National Reserve Association (later renamed the Federal Reserve Association), which would be a voluntary, regional association of banks supervised by a national body elected by bankers.

These associations would have the power to manage reserves and issue currency.

The plan is believed to have been drafted not by Senator Aldrich, but by Paul Warburg[12] – a representative of the Rothschilds, who ran the largest banking firm in Europe. This was done in consultation with several other political and financial luminaries of the time, including Assistant Secretary of the Treasury Abraham Pitt Andrew; President of the National City Bank of New York, Frank Vanderlip; Senior partner of the J.P. Morgan Company, Henry P. Davison; President of Morgan's First National Bank of New York, Charles Norton; Head of Morgan's Bankers Trust Company, Benjamin Strong; and Warburg himself. These men met in secret for a week in 1911 at the island resort of Jekyll Island, GA because they thought that any knowledge of leading bankers getting together to draft a banking bill would be doomed to failure in Congress. Some historians believe the purpose of this secret meeting and the ultimate formation of the Federal Reserve was to form a banking cartel. The theory that these titans of finance would meet to form such a cartel is not too outlandish, considering the times. Several industries formed groups to protect their interests, including rail roads, oil, steel and other manufacturers. The groups sought to limit new competition and to maintain higher prices for their products. Aldrich presented 'his' proposal for the banking industry to the National Monetary Commission in January 1911[13].

The campaign for public support was based on several points including:

- To keep up with other major economies in the world that had central banks,
- To prevent irresponsible bankers from expanding too much,
- To stop inflationary tendencies,
- To function as a lender of last resort and expand money supply and credit to ensure that banks didn't fail the way they had, and
- To ensure that money supply was 'elastic': i.e., to expand money supply and credit during a recession or banking panic.

The Aldrich Plan was never put to a vote as opponents, including President Woodrow Wilson and his Secretary of State, William Jennings Bryan, cited the lack of government control over the proposed body resulting in too much power concentrated in the hands of a select few bankers, the so-called 'money trust'.[14] Other reasons cited were its 'dangerous monopolistic aspects' and the danger of inflation inherent in the proposed system.

The Birth of the Federal Reserve System

With the clamor for financial reform continuing, the Owen-Glass[15] Bill was drafted by Congressman Carter Glass. It was similar to the Aldrich Plan in suggesting the establishment of regional reserve banks that would function as central banks in their respective regions and issue federal currency against reserves of gold and commercial paper. President Wilson insisted on the addition of a federal board that would control and manage the activities of these regional banks.

The result was the proposed Federal Reserve System of 12 fairly autonomous regional reserve banks that would be owned by chartered regional banks and governed by a Federal Reserve Board. The board would be appointed by the President and would include two ex-officio members, the Treasury Secretary and the Comptroller of Currency. Moreover, all banks with national charters had to be members of their respective regional banks. The system was publicized as being privately owned, yet publicly controlled.

There were also a couple of notable revisions made to the draft Glass-Owen bill. **One of the most important points in Senator Owen's original draft was the requirement that the Federal Reserve maintain stable money.** A concern on the part of many legislators was the potential a central bank would have in creating an excess of capital thereby generating inflation. However, the requirement to maintain stable money was deleted before the Bill was put to vote.

Through another notable revision, the bill also reduced reserve requirements for banks, which previously required banks to maintain a 20% reserve. After the new system went into effect, this requirement was cut to just 10% allowing banks to lend a greater portion of each dollar on deposit. This move made inflation more likely due to the fact banks would likely increase their lending activities increasing the supply of money in the system. The Bill was finally approved by Congress and signed into law by President Woodrow Wilson on December 23, 1913 as the Federal Reserve Act.

The Federal Reserve System was given a powerful mandate. It has a monopoly over the country's currency issuance and it controls the supply of money in the national economy. Among other duties, it is also supposed to manipulate the supply of money and credit in order to:

1. Ensure sustainable growth,
2. Maintain high employment levels,
3. Maintain stable prices, and
4. Moderate long-term interest rates.

There are 12 regional Federal Reserve Banks[16] under the Federal Reserve System which is considered a private entity within the government, but subject to oversight by Congress. (It apprises Congress of its activities twice a year).

Perhaps the most important and far-reaching consequence of the formation of the Federal Reserve was a gradual shifting of the US to a diluted and denatured gold standard – a fractional reserve system ultimately based on fiat money whose issuance was controlled by the Federal Reserve. In effect, this legislated away the free market with respect to the supply of money and credit, passing the responsibility on to central bankers and their member banks.

Fiat Money in America

The American War of Independence was financed not by gold-backed money, but by fiat money – Continentals – from which the phrase "not worth a Continental" was derived, signifying something that is worthless. Continentals were eventually redeemed for 1/100th of their original value. The founding fathers had experienced the damage fiat money had caused to the economy, and George Washington even contributed his own silver for the initial coins minted to insure the adoption of a hard currency system. The US Coinage Act of 1792 provided for a US Mint, which stamped silver and gold coins. One dollar was defined by statute as a specific weight of gold.

The United States continued using a gold-backed currency until 1862 when it shifted temporarily to a fiat money system to finance the Civil War. This time, the government issued Greenbacks, which were redeemable in gold at a future, unspecified date. It took the country 30 years to move back to full gold exchangeability and when it did so, prices stayed stable. Except for the brief periods in America described earlier, there was practically zero inflation between 1792 and 1914. Price levels based on gold were remarkably stable. However, in the aftermath of WWI, there was simply not enough gold around to back the amount of currency needed to pay for the war. One by one, countries de-linked their currencies from gold.

Advantages of a Gold Standard

Under a gold standard, it is nearly impossible to make large federal borrowings or to operate with large sustained budget deficits. Such a standard also limited the number of dollar claims that could be issued. If the government needed more money, it would have to either reduce expenditures or raise taxes. What limited ability the government would have for issuance of bonds would compete for and crowd out private debt issuance. US government bond issuance would drain the pool of investment dollars, driving interest rates higher, until additional investment dollars would become attracted to the higher yields. It is precisely the absence of this limitation and market discipline that allows governments to run up budget deficits by printing money that is backed by nothing tangible, forcing future generations to pay the bill.

How the Federal Reserve creates money out of thin air

With Federal Reserve banking, more money can be loaned out than actually exists in reserve. Money is 'created' by posting a new loan on the balance sheet and is given out in the form of banknotes issued by the central bank to a member bank. It can then be used as cash and loaned out to borrowers.

To better illustrate what happens in the process of money and credit creation, imagine an island nation with 10 inhabitants, each with $1,000 in the bank for a total money supply of $10,000. One individual gets sunburned and the government feels sorry for him, deciding to give him $1,000 to match his existing savings. The government can do one of three things to fund the payment. First, it can tax the inhabitants $100 each and pay the victim $1,000. The victim now has $1,900 after paying his $100 tax, while his countrymen are left with $900 each. The total money supply of the island remains at $10,000.

Another option would be to issue a bond to another inhabitant to fund the $1,000 payment. Assuming a citizen buys the bond from the government, he will have spent his money, leaving him without funds to make purchases for a time. Again, money supply remains at $10,000, as one inhabitant has $2,000, one has 0 and 8 have $1,000 each.

In the third scenario, the government issues a bond for $1,000, but instead of selling it to an investor, the Federal Reserve Bank buys it. Even though the Fed has no money, it has been decreed that it can create it. So the Fed buys the bond from the government, writing it a check for $1,000 with which to pay the citizen. Now one citizen has $2,000 and 9 have $1,000 for a total money supply of $11,000. Since all the inhabitants are smart capitalists, they rush out and get sunburned so they too can increase their savings. The government obligingly pays each his $1,000 and the Federal Reserve dutifully buys the bonds issued by the government. Everyone now has $2,000 and the island's money supply has increased to $20,000 without any change to productivity. However, with twice as many dollars, the purchasing power of each dollar has been reduced by 50%. In other words, prices for goods and services will double. If the only food left on the island for the next few days was one fish, there would be twice as much money bid on it.

The value of goods and services are calibrated in relation to each other. If the man who repairs huts for $10 per hour earns the equivalent of 10 coconuts at $1 each, he will react to an overnight doubling of the money supply by keeping his fee commensurate with the price of coconuts and other goods and services. The repairman would charge $20 per hour and the price of coconuts would be raised to $2 each, which still nets him 10 coconuts per hour.

After the Federal Reserve was established, bankers could increase money supply beyond the safety margin of the fractional reserve. Economist **Murray Rothbard** calls the structure of the Fed and the corresponding banking structure an 'inflationary structure' that subsequently fueled the credit boom of the 1920s (induced by the inherent structure of a fractional reserve system).

After recovering from the financial drain of the First World War, the world returned not to a gold standard but a **Gold Exchange Standard,** wherein each country pegged its currency to the US dollar, which in turn was pegged to gold. The mid-1920s, however, was also a time when the Federal Reserve rapidly expanded money supply. Between 1921 and 1929, money supply expanded from $45 billion to $73 billion, an approximate 7% annualized inflation in the supply of money. Since the currency in circulation component of money supply remained constant during that period, the increase in money supply was attributable to money substitutes through the expansion of credits. One factor causing the expansion resulted from the then recently signed Federal Reserve Act, which allowed banks to start paying interest on time deposits (similar to today's CDs). Due to the fact demand deposits (similar to today's checking accounts) required a larger 10% reserve backing and time deposits required only 3%, the bank naturally encouraged its customers to utilize time deposits so it could lend out more money and thus earn more profits. Open market purchases of Treasury bonds by Federal Reserve Chairman Benjamin Strong, along with the de facto reduction in reserve requirements, helped to cause interest rates to artificially move to levels that were lower than where the free market levels would have been.

The inflation of liquidity oddly enough did not raise consumer price inflation – it changed little throughout the decade of the 1920s. However, in analyzing the impact of monetary inflation one must observe where the funds are directed. In the 1920s it was directed to speculators in the stock market and real estate, and to the capital goods sector. 90% margin loans were extended to stock market speculators, helping to send the market significantly higher. The Dow Jones Industrial Average rocketed from approximately 100 in 1920 to almost 400 at its peak in 1929. Real estate also went through a boom period, led by Florida properties. With regard to capital investment, as the money available carried artificially low rates, over-investment in plant and equipment resulted.

This misapplication of artificially cheap funds caused a change in the structure of production, disrupting the normal equilibrium between costs and prices. Once an artificial flow of funds ceases or reverses, the projected rates of return are not realized. This may help to explain why monetary inflation in the 1920s did not lead to consumer price inflation. Plant capacity had over-expanded, which in turn satisfied increased demand for goods at subdued prices. The fact that monetary inflation does not always correlate to price inflation, yet can still impart devastating results that are manifested in other areas of the economy, should be noted when evaluating our current economic environment.

Finally, in late 1928, the Fed started tightening money supply by selling government securities to banks, thus draining funds available to lend to the public. The Fed wanted to slow an overheated economy and rein in the runaway stock market. Interest rates climbed from 3.5% to 5% in a matter of months. By this time, however, the imbalances (excessively high stock markets, real estate markets and plant capacity) were so severe that the Fed's actions led to a collapse in the stock market, which crashed in October 1929. By 1931, the Fed had even stopped functioning as a lender of last resort and stood by while a general bank run ensued. Banks, without the benefit of the FDIC to insure deposits, folded one after the other throughout the country. Other factors such as protectionist trade legislation and a drought in the farm belt known as "The Dustbowl" also played roles in worsening the subsequent depression. But, the chain of events of a loose credit environment, the distortions it caused, and the necessary, but overdue tightening of money supply to correct the previous monetary policy mistakes, undoubtedly played a major role in causing the Great Depression.

The US Dollar Becomes Pure Fiat Money

The Great Depression set the stage for the arrival of big government and the welfare state. It also led to public support for the demonetization of gold because the rigidity of sound money had been partially blamed for the country's economic condition. As part of his New Deal to take America out of its depression, President Roosevelt demonetized gold in April 1933. The gold standard was removed, outlawing the redemption of Federal Reserve notes that until then were redeemable in gold. (Foreign central banks, however, could still convert their dollar holdings into gold.) Roosevelt knew that the ability to redeem money for gold prevented the system from printing the additional money he felt was needed to pay for large government deficits and expenditures that the proposed new welfare state needed. It became illegal for US citizens to hold gold in any form other than jewelry and rare collectable coins. The Emergency Banking Act forced Americans to convert their gold coins, gold certificates and bullion into US dollars at the rate of $20.67 per ounce. Roosevelt justified this by saying that people were hoarding gold which served no useful purpose. That the dollar had been severely overvalued verses gold was obvious when in less than a year, the US government revalued gold from $20.67 an ounce to $35 an ounce, making the dollar worth 40% less than it had been.

Bretton Woods and the Dollar Standard

Representatives of developed countries met in July 1944 in the New Hampshire town of Bretton Woods to develop a new international monetary system. The Bretton Woods Accord established a gold exchange standard – but this too was a 'denatured' gold standard – with both the US dollar and the British pound[17]. The international value of a nation's currency was determined by its fixed relationship to the dollar, which in turn was fixed to gold, which was to be used to settle international accounts. The gold standard maintained fixed exchange rates and pegged the US dollar to gold at $35 an ounce – the rate at which the dollar was exchangeable to gold.

Rothbard says that the US motive behind establishing Bretton Woods was to "reconstruct the international monetary system from the conflicting currency blocs of the 1930s into a new form of international gold exchange standard. This new form...closely resembled the...British system of the 1920s. The difference is that the world fiat currencies now pyramided on top of the dollar reserves kept in New York instead of the sterling reserve kept in London."[18]

The US was the only country that emerged from World War II wealthier than when it had entered it. In 1946, it possessed about $26 billion in gold, while all the rest of the countries in the world combined held only $7 billion in gold. The US not only accounted for two-thirds of the world's money supply, but also half of the world's productive capacity and nearly one-quarter of international trade. It was the world's leading exporter and needed the foreign demand that the ravaged economic landscapes of Europe and the developing world readily provided. The U.S. dollar came to function as the international reserve currency and it benefited the most from the Bretton Woods Accord because other countries, in essence, provided unlimited financing to the U.S. as a result of their new need to hold dollar assets.

The Fed Goes Off the Gold Standard

The Bretton Woods system worked well for the US until 1958 when the country experienced a balance of payments deficit for the first time since the end of WWII. At first perceived as temporary, foreign governments began to worry when the deficit continued into the next decade as the US struggled to finance the Vietnam War. The decline in America's international reserve assets was combined with an equally damaging increase in its liabilities to foreign central banks. The Fed began printing billions of dollars creating a worldwide dollar glut.

There were also subtle shifts in the nature of money in the US. Federal Reserve notes released in 1963 made no promise to pay in "lawful money" as had been the practice in the past. Two years later, silver was completely eliminated from all US coins except the Kennedy half-dollar, which contained only 40 percent silver. President Lyndon B. Johnson signed the Coinage Act of 1965[19]; terminating legislation signed by George Washington, and allowed the US Treasury to remove the silver content from the nation's currency.

In 1965, French President Charles de Gaulle asked for approximately

$200 million that France held to be converted into gold. The US honored its commitment since foreign central banks were allowed to convert dollars into gold at the official price of $35 an ounce. This was a clear signal that the world had serious misgivings as to the value of the dollar and that other central banks would soon follow France's lead.

In 1967, President Johnson declared that the world supply of gold was insufficient to make the system workable. The following June, he issued a proclamation that all Federal Reserve Silver Certificates were merely fiat legal tender and could not be redeemed in silver. Things continued to worsen as the budget deficit reached WWII levels the following year.

Between January and June of 1971, assets worth $22 billion left the country. Foreign holders of the US dollar were losing faith in the currency and America's ability to cut its massive budget and trade deficits. So many dollars were being created that foreign central bankers rightly believed that the dollars they held were worth less than the gold which they could receive in exchange from the Fed.

In August 1971, President Nixon unilaterally "closed the gold window," reneging on America's promise to pay foreign central banks gold in return for their dollar reserves. It was the end of the international gold exchange standard. The period from 1971 to the present is the longest time in history that the world has functioned without any kind of gold standard[20]. The severing of the gold link in 1971 and the movement to flexible exchange rates removed the constraints on monetary expansion. US government T-bills and bonds became a new form of international money. The new, elastic international money supply also served to accommodate the supply shock of the first oil crisis at the end of 1973. The Fed accelerated its money creation, hoping that the announced end of the Vietnam War would ease the deficits. Instead, deficits continued to grow and bank credit expanded at double-digit rates as prices soared.

By the end of the 1970s, America faced both runaway inflation and a recession; unemployment was rising and productivity was declining. In 1979, the second oil crisis took inflation to a post-war record high of 11.3%. In response, President Jimmy Carter nominated Paul Volker as Chairman of the Federal Reserve Board to tackle this 'stagflation'.

Paul Volker

Volker, who had earlier served as Treasury Department Undersecretary under Nixon, took an aggressive stance against inflation. His attack on inflation was twofold. First, the Fed has the right to order, through open-market operations, the purchase and sales of government bonds from its own account against the accounts of member banks. When the Fed *buys* government securities for its own account, there is a corresponding issuance of capital to the banks that they tend to lend out to borrowers. In essence, the Fed creates money with its 'magic checkbook', infusing money into the system, similar to the example of the island nation. Volker, however, did just the reverse: he *sold* government bonds the Federal Reserve was holding to the member banks in exchange for capital that would no longer be available for loan to the public.

Second, the Fed also raised the Fed funds and discount rates[21]. At one point, short-term yields were as high as 20% while the discount rate touched 14%. This was a highly unpopular move since the higher interest rates sent the economy into a deeper recession. Business people, consumers and politicians alike protested the move. Volker also faced criticism from high-ranking members of the Reagan administration. Inflation stood at over 13% at the end of 1981 and unemployment hit 10%. It was considered to be the worst recession since the Great Depression, but Volker remained resolute and kept money supply tight even through the first half of 1982. In essence, he maintained higher real interest rates until it suppressed both inflation and inflationary psychology.

Although the pain was substantial, Volker's decision proved to be the right one as he broke the back of inflation and established faith that the dollar's value would be protected. His assertive stance was almost a proxy for the strong discipline that a gold backed currency would instill in an economy.

In late 1982, correctly sensing that inflationary psychology was wrung out of the system, Volker expanded money supply and lowered the discount rate from 11% to 8.5%. In the following months, the economy was revived and expanded just as he had anticipated. His staunchest critics had been silenced by the results of the bitter pill he had doled out to the American economy.

Moving forward under the Reagan administration, America became competitive once again. But the billions spent on the Strategic Defense Initiative, among other things, caused the budget deficit to soar. Big tax cuts were not offset by the increase in tax revenues from economic growth as expected. As budget deficits increased, the dollar began to fall in value. Once again Volker began to raise interest rates; this continued until his retirement in 1987.

Alan Greenspan

When Alan Greenspan took over as Volker's replacement, he continued raising interest rates until October 1987 when the stock market crashed. Greenspan and the Fed responded to the crash by flooding Wall Street with much-needed liquidity and the markets steadied. Thus began Greenspan's tenure as the longest-serving chairman of the Federal Reserve Board.

Greenspan had begun his career as a follower of novelist-philosopher Ayn Rand's Objectivist principles, believing in sound money and opposing big government. He was, in fact, an ardent champion of the gold standard and its merits. In a much-quoted 1967 essay he wrote: "The financial policy of the welfare state requires that there be no way for the owners of wealth to protect themselves. This is the shabby secret of the welfare statists' tirades against gold. Deficit spending is simply a scheme for the confiscation of wealth. Gold stands in the way of this insidious process. It stands as a protector of property rights."[22]

He also wrote passionately about how an unjustified increase in money supply creates inflation and erodes the value of the currency. "As the supply of money (of claims) increases relative to the supply of tangible assets in the economy, prices must eventually rise. Thus the earnings saved by the productive members of the society lose value in terms of goods. When the economy's books are finally balanced, one finds that this loss in value represents the goods purchased by the government for welfare or other purposes with the money proceeds of the government bonds financed by bank credit expansion."

When Greenspan became Fed Chairman, it was widely believed that he would put the Federal Reserve on a course that would at least mimic the restraints of a gold standard by limiting the monetary growth rate. His predecessor had already put that policy in place. After the injection of funds into the economy following the stock market crash of 1987, Greenspan did follow that policy for a while, but more or less stopped after the early 1990s. After that, Greenspan's Fed – except for short periods of time – pumped the economy with more money than can be justified by its rate of growth.

There were periods where he did raise interest rates to curb inflationary tendencies. In 1994, for example, he raised interest rates, helping to prevent speculative excesses. However, after this came a period that witnessed some spectacular financial failures and the beginning of an era that would see some of the largest bailouts ever organized by the Federal Reserve.

In the 1960s, Greenspan had correctly explained: "In the absence of the gold standard, there is no way to protect savings from confiscation through inflation. There is no safe store of value. The abandonment of the gold standard made it possible for welfare statists to use the banking system as a means to an unlimited expansion of credit (debt creation)."[23] However, from the late 1990s to 2006, the same Alan Greenspan presided over one of the largest explosions of money supply and credit excess brought on by sustained low interest rates. Greenspan's actions promoted leveraged speculation and mortgage borrowings as tools to reflate the economy after the tech bubble burst at the turn of the century - a simple case of short-term expediency causing long-term consequences.

In 2002, Greenspan went on record admitting that the abandonment of the gold standard had caused a severe increase in money supply: "It was the case that the price level in 1929 was not much different, on net, from what it had been in 1800. But, in the two decades following the abandonment of the gold standard in 1933, the consumer price index in the United States nearly doubled. And, in the four decades after that, prices quintupled. Monetary policy, unleashed from the constraint of the domestic currency's convertibility into gold, has allowed a persistent over-issuance of money. As recently as a decade ago, central bankers, having witnessed more than a half-century of chronic inflation, appeared to confirm that a fiat currency was inherently subject to excess."[24] Since the US went on a pure fiat money standard in 1971, money supply has increased approximately 12-fold.

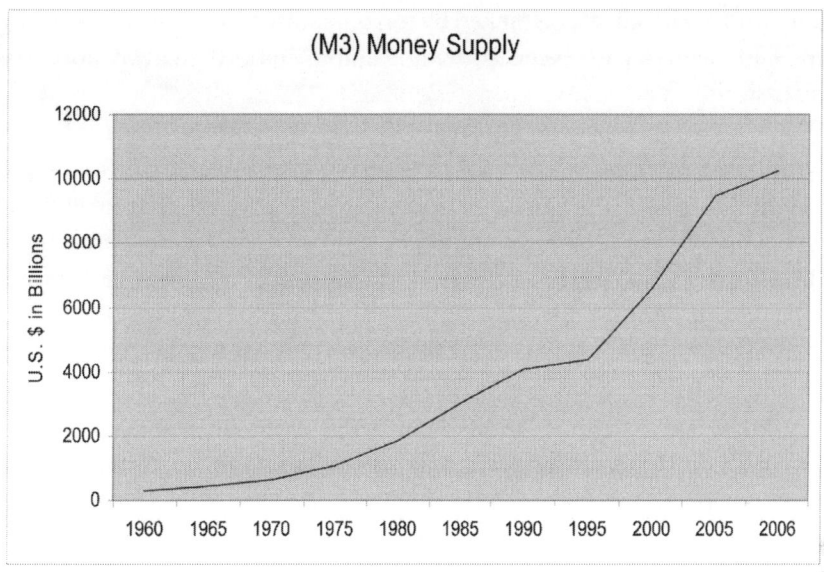

Source: Federal Reserve Data

At the same time in 2002, Greenspan told a House Financial Affairs Committee that the Fed had been acting as if it were on the gold standard after learning its lesson during the inflationary crises of the 1970s. However, there is no evidence that the Fed was acting as if it were on the gold standard – in fact, there is evidence to the contrary.

By Greenspan's own admission, money supply has expanded rapidly ever since the US began facing balance of payment problems in the 1960s. The M3 figure for September 1960 was $310.4 billion, which took 10 years to double to $652.7 billion in 1970. However, this figure almost doubled again to $1.14 trillion by 1975 – the period when inflation was at its worst. The M3 figure when Greenspan retired in 2006 was a staggering $10.3 trillion or more than twice the 1995 level.

Bernanke's Helicopter Money to Fight Deflation

In the past few years there were many seemingly good reasons to inflate the nation's money supply to avert crises. In 1994 the Mexican peso collapsed, in 1998 there was an Asian currency crisis, Russian debt default and a major hedge fund (Long Term Capital Management) collapse. In 1999 fears ran high regarding the impact of Y2K on the nation's computers. From 2000 to 2002, the US stock market plunged, and in 2001 the US was attacked by terrorists. In each of these instances, the Fed raced to the rescue, providing ample liquidity to avert potential recessions.

There are, however, consequences involved in the Fed's inflation of the money supply. One is the erosion of purchasing power, discussed earlier. Another is the accumulation of bad investments that takes place when money is artificially abundant and inexpensive to come by. A third consequence is the moral hazard that occurs among investors and speculators. Moral hazard describes the riskier behavior an individual demonstrates due to his perception that if a negative outcome occurs, he will be bailed out. If a person has fire insurance, he is less likely to buy a fire extinguisher. Similarly, a hedge fund manager, comforted by the belief that the Fed will bail out the economy if an unforeseen situation or event threatens the financial markets, is less apt to place as much weight on that negative circumstance and thereby invest more aggressively than he would have in the absence of such a belief. An accumulation of such risk behavior can cause greater risk to the financial system.

We have discussed the various mandates for which the Fed is responsible. With respect to stable prices, for the last few decades, the Fed has talked about preventing inflation. There is a growing concern among some economists, however, that deflating prices may be a cause for concern in the future. Current Fed chairman Ben Bernanke has expressed his concerns over deflationary monetary policy in the US during the 1930s and in Japan during the 1990s[25].

One must differentiate between monetary and price deflation just as that differentiation exists with monetary and price inflation. In a sound money based, normally functioning, capitalistic economy, a slight deflation in prices is common. Advancements in technology and innovation allow corporations to reduce costs and improve the quality of their products and services over time. If a corporation decides not to pass the cost savings on to its customers, competitors rush in to exploit the higher profit margins until prices and margins are driven lower. As described earlier, monetary inflation increases the number of dollars outstanding, decreasing the value of each dollar. More depreciated dollars are required to pay for a particular item than with a stable monetary regime. Monetary deflation on the other hand, decreases the available dollars in the economy. With fewer dollars, consumers are less likely to spend, causing a decline in prices and dampening of economic activity. Monetary deflation is lethal to those who have large debts because dollars become scarce, making it harder to gather them to pay back debts.

Although I believe the analytical focus should be on the loose money, inflationary policies leading up to their respective crisis points, the devastating consequences monetary deflation had during the US depression in the 1930s and the prolonged Japanese recession of the 1990s is not in dispute. But, an attempt to continue inflating our way out of trouble can have devastating consequences of its own. Theoretically, an inflationary-minded Fed could buy all the government securities in sight and potentially delve into other securities such as mortgage-backed securities, corporate bonds and stocks. The Fed could, in effect, create trillions of new dollars for financial institutions to lend. This activity, however, would cause the dollar to plunge in value, which would translate into skyrocketing prices of goods and services, under this extreme scenario. Foreign investors' losses on US assets would mount as the exchange value of the dollar plummets. Meanwhile, savings in the US would be destroyed as the purchasing power of saved dollars declines. Millions of people who are retired or close to retirement, having saved money throughout their lives, would suddenly lack the means to pay for higher everyday expenses.

Extreme situations require extreme measures. In our current environment, we have an unprecedented amount of debt owed by government and consumers, a fiat currency that is not tethered to anything real and a Federal Reserve chairman who has resolved to prevent deflation. Over time, more and more inflation will be required to sustain the economy. The bigger the beast gets the more nourishment it requires. This sets the stage for a hyperinflationary environment that runs out of control. Just as with deflation, hyperinflation can lead to devastating consequences as it did for Germany post WWI or for Argentina in the 1990s, as discussed in Chapter 1.

In the absence of a true gold standard, the only tolerable substitute is a proactive Fed that consistently behaves in the manner Alan Greenspan described early in his tenure, whereby the Fed acts as if a gold standard was in place. In this way, the Fed would be able to prevent the monetary inflation that must later be corrected. The longer it goes uncorrected, the more bitter the correction will be later on.

Ben Bernanke's now infamous "printing press" speech (made when he was a Governor on the Federal Reserve Board) talked of a potential deflation and how, unlike in the past when the gold standard 'interfered' with easy solutions, this time the Fed was prepared with a "new technology": that of the electronic printing presses which could print up as many dollars as the Fed orders[26]. In another reference to the expansion of money supply the Fed could engineer, he talked about doing the equivalent of a "helicopter drop of money" in the face of deflation. "By increasing the number of US dollars in circulation," said Bernanke, "or even by credibly threatening to do so, the US government can also reduce the value of a dollar in terms of goods and services, which is equivalent to raising the prices in dollars of those goods and services... under a paper-money system, a determined government can always generate higher spending and positive inflation....If we do fall into deflation...we can take comfort that the logic of the printing press example must assert itself, and sufficient injections of money will ultimately always reverse a deflation."[27]

Bernanke – an Ivy League academician– is already well known for his research and views on the Fed's role in causing and prolonging the Great Depression. He asserts that by raising interest rates in a weakened economy without any evident price inflation, the Fed caused price deflation and surging unemployment. The error was compounded, he wrote, by creating a credit crunch when banks were failing[28]. His conclusion trivializes the loose money, inflationary policies that led to the problems and imbalances the country faced in the late 1920s. In addition he failed to discuss the drawbacks to continuing the inflationary policies through the 1930s. Perhaps, for a while, the nation would have been better off with inflation rather than deflation in the 1930s, but what would happen next? An extension of the rising trend of stock and real estate markets, and a continued increase in plant capacity, beyond sustainable levels, would have only lead to greater distortions eventually requiring reconciliation.

But in 2006, our economy was already flush with money and credit. To foreign investors and central banks loaded with massive quantities of dollar-denominated investments, the imagery of rushing helicopters and printing presses is chilling. Bernanke's 'helicopter money' comment may be remembered when a foreign central banker is faced with the decision to continue recycling his export-generated dollars back into US dollar-denominated investments as those investments pile up. Or if he is once again asked to intervene in the event of a financial crisis by buying additional US paper.

An artificially prolonged expansion – like the one we faced in 2007 – creates an environment where weak companies stay in business, affecting healthy companies, and consumers continue to spend beyond their means because they come to believe that times will always be good. Investors end up speculating with greater amounts of money in riskier and riskier ventures, further inflating asset bubbles.

In the midst of all this, Bernanke's contention – once again mirroring Greenspan's – is that the yawning US deficit is the result of a 'global savings glut'[29]. The explanation is that foreign investors have rushed to invest in US assets thanks to greater safety and liquidity, and returns to be earned from our real estate, stocks and bonds. This action consequently finances the US budget and trade deficits, keeping interest rates low, which results in more spending.

The Bank for International Settlements issues reports on purchases of US assets by both foreign private investors and foreign central banks. Foreign central banks are not as sensitive to returns as private investors; they are sensitive to maintaining a stronger dollar so they can competitively export goods. Private foreign investors are sensitive to returns, so any negative shift in perception in the sustainability of a strong dollar could generate a flood of dollar asset selling from them. Foreign central banks invested $200 billion in US assets in 2005 and almost $400 billion in 2004, while private foreign investors invested $1 trillion in 2005 and slightly over that in 2004. Comments by policymakers, such as those made by Bernanke, are surely being scrutinized by the foreign entities that hold so much of our debt and rely on a stable, protected dollar to prevent losses on their investments.

From the late 1960s to 1971, foreign nations holding dollars doubted the soundness of the currency and asked for it to be converted to gold. Today, if China and Japan (who between them hold over a trillion dollars of US debt) begin doubting the soundness of the dollar, they cannot ask for their dollars to be converted to gold. But they could stop buying our debt or even sell off some of their existing US holdings. That kind of action could send US interest rates soaring, driving down the value of both Treasuries and the dollar.

Foreign buying has not stopped yet through the first half of 2006, but there is a growing uneasiness as foreign central banks discuss diversifying their reserves into greater weightings of other foreign currencies and gold. Although this action might negatively impact their export competitiveness, the alternative of sustaining large currency translation losses on existing and new US dollar-denominated purchases looms large.

Chapter 3

The Role of Financial Intermediaries

The Federal Reserve Board enjoyed much greater control over the financial system and credit creation in the past than they do now. Although it still sets the tone in terms of cost and availability of credit, other institutions outside the banking system are playing a more significant role than in past years. Technology and globalization have ushered in an era where foreign governments and institutions are much more active in buying, selling, lending and borrowing within the US capital markets. The impact of the globalization of our markets will be discussed in greater detail in Chapter 5. This chapter will focus on a domestic element outside the banking system whose influence over our financial markets has grown exponentially in recent years, that of the financial intermediaries. A financial intermediary is a firm that indirectly channels funds between lenders and borrowers. These financial institutions greatly influence the availability of credit in the economy.

Securitization

There are a variety of types of financial institutions established to raise money at one interest rate then lend that money to others at a higher interest rate, earning a profit based on the spread between those rates. For example, a consumer finance company can issue loans to individuals purchasing television sets. The finance company may then hold the loans or create securities by packaging the television loans and selling them to investors in a process known as securitization. Securitization involves the creation of financial instruments which are backed by cash flows that are specifically pledged to repay the principal and interest of these securities. It is a structured finance technique that converts a portfolio of assets (loans) into tradable securities. A security is more marketable if the underlying loans share certain attributes such as the type of loan, expected maturity, interest rate, etc. The process of securitization serves to monetize the finance company's loan holdings, freeing up capital to make additional loans. It also serves to transfer the risk of default on television buyers' debt to those investing in these newly created securities, unless the finance company guarantees the loan payments, in which case it would earn a larger fee. The finance company collects loan payments from the television buyers, retains a servicing fee, and then pays the rest to the investors.

These types of securities are known as asset-backed securities (ABS) and collectively amounted to a market value of nearly $2 trillion in 2005, a sixfold increase since 1995, according to the Bond Market Association. ABSs can be categorized by the loans they contain. The most common are home equity loans, credit card receivables, collateralized bond obligations, auto loans, student loans, equipment leases and manufactured housing loans[30]. Pools of home mortgages are similarly constructed and called mortgage-backed securities (MBS) and commanded a market value of over $6 trillion at the beginning of 2006.

Consumer finance companies can be either captive (part of a larger company) or independent. Captive finance companies such as GMAC, Ford Motor Credit and GE Credit were intended to assist in the sale of products made by their respective parent companies. However, in many instances the finance units of large companies generate more profits than the core manufacturing segments of the companies.

Major financial institutions are also involved in the production of credits and debits, often through captive subsidiaries. Brokerage firms, insurance companies and government sponsored entities (GSEs) are all major players. We will discuss the GSEs because of the enormous size these institutions collectively represent and the systemic risk they introduce.

Government Sponsored Entities (GSE)

GSEs are privately held organizations created by the US Congress to increase the liquidity and lower the cost of capital for certain sectors of the economy. The largest sector beneficiary is housing, but loans to farmers are also favorably impacted.

The following are the five government sponsored enterprises (GSEs) in the U.S.

1. Federal National Mortgage Association (Fannie Mae)
2. Federal Home Loan Mortgage Corporation (Freddie Mac)
3. Federal Home Loan Banks
4. Federal Agricultural Mortgage Corporation (Farmer Mac)
5. Federal Farm Credit System

The largest of the GSEs is Fannie Mae, which along with its smaller sibling, Freddie Mac, does not lend money directly to homeowners. Instead, mortgage loans are originated by banking and savings and loan institutions. If a bank makes a loan that conforms to certain guidelines established by Fannie Mae (conforming loan), it can have Fannie guarantee the repayment of principal and interest on the loan for a fee. The conforming loan guidelines are subject to change, but involve a borrower's credit score, monthly expense to income ratio, monthly expense plus debt service to income ratio and funds to close percentage (generally 20%). A limit is imposed annually to the overall loan amount; this was set at $417,000 for 2006.

The bank can choose to hold the newly guaranteed loans itself or package them together and sell them, usually to Fannie Mae directly, for cash. The bank that originated the loan can continue to maintain a relationship with the borrower, collecting the monthly mortgage payments. However, since the bank has either insured or sold the loan, there is a lack of accountability on the part of the lender. As long as the borrower conforms to the guidelines laid down by Fannie Mae, the bank is not penalized for non-performance on the borrower's part. The day of the skeptical, stone-faced lending officer, whose survival depended on making loans to people who made good on their promise to pay the money back is over.

The History of the GSEs

Fannie Mae was created by congress during the Great Depression in 1938. Its purpose was to bolster the housing industry by providing liquidity to FHA-backed mortages, and later, to VA mortgages sold by banking institutions. Having suffered great losses during the depression, banks were reluctant to lend money to the housing industry. However, the FHA guaranteed certain housing loans, removing risk for the banks, and Fannie Mae provided liquidity by purchasing the insured loans from the banks so they could in turn use the cash to originate new loans.

Congress stipulated certain responsibilities in granting a charter to Fannie Mae. One duty was to provide stability and liquidity in the secondary market for residential mortgages. An additional role was to improve the distribution of investment capital available for residential lending to low- and moderate-income families and to families living in urban, rural and other underserved areas.

In 1968, due to budget constraints, the government partitioned Fannie Mae into two separate entities. One of the entities, Ginnie Mae, was formed to handle most of the government policy tasks and to provide a secondary market for government-insured loans (FHA and VA). Ginnie Mae remains a government entity and its debt continues to enjoy the full faith and credit of the US government.

The other entity to emerge from the 1968 restructure retained the name Fannie Mae and was moved off budget and established as a shareholder-owned entity. Fannie Mae's role shifted to guaranteeing non-government insured mortgage loans (non-FHA and non-VA). Since the new Fannie was shareholder-owned rather than government-owned like Ginnie Mae, it did not enjoy the full faith and credit of the US government, which continues to be true today, contrary to what many believe. Later, Freddie Mac was similarly created as a private company to promote liquidity in the secondary market for mortgages originated by savings and loans. Like Fannie Mae, Freddie Mac's debt is not guaranteed by the government.

Favors Afforded the GSEs

The new charter required Fannie to be financed by private capital, yet continue to provide stability and liquidity in the secondary market for residential mortgages, particularly with respect to families in low-income brackets and underserved areas. Since it became a shareholder entity, management was faced with serving two masters, the government with its mandates and the shareholders who own the company. In return for adherence to the government mandates, Fannie and Freddie were granted certain privileges, which they still enjoy today. The primary advantages afforded them were as follows:

Providing access to capital markets

The focus of these institutions has predominantly been to reduce interest rates on loans for exclusive borrowing groups. The GSEs' support for this type of debt allows it to be much more liquid, attracting institutional interest from hedge funds, insurance companies, domestic and international banks, pension funds, mutual funds, foundations and others. One might argue that the nature of these fragmented loan markets makes it more difficult to attract institutional investors in the absence of the GSEs. The act of pooling loans that conform to certain standardized criteria, stamping the loans with a GSE guarantee, then developing the securities so they are homogeneous regarding certain characteristics, serves to commoditize these loans, making them more liquid. Deep markets and enhanced liquidity attract larger investment entities, which helps to drive down the interest rates associated with these securities. One could make a case, however, that the free market could accomplish what the GSEs have by substituting private insurance for GSE insurance.

Implicit guarantee by the federal government

GSEs operate with a distinct advantage over their privately instituted competitors with similar balance sheet strength, mainly due to an implicit government guarantee extended to these agencies' debt. The operative word is implicit or implied; these debts are not explicitly guaranteed by the government. The US Treasury guarantees a line of credit for Fannie Mae and Freddie Mac for up to $2.25 billion each, an amount dwarfed by a multi-trillion dollar mortgage market. It is assumed by the markets that in the event there is trouble in the mortgage bond market and the GSEs' financial viability is at stake, the government would decide to rescue them because they are simply "too big to fail". Alan Greenspan has said: "Although prospectuses of GSE debt are required by law to stipulate that such instruments are not backed by the full faith and credit of the US government, investors worldwide have concluded that our government will not allow GSEs to default. As a consequence, market participants offer to purchase GSE debt at interest rates substantially lower than those required of comparably situated financial institutions without direct ties to government."[31] Debt securities issued by the GSEs are rated AAA/Aaa by the rating services Moody's and Standard and Poor's. The implicit credit subsidy is estimated to save the GSEs over $6 billion per year in interest costs.[32]

Tax exemption and SEC exemption

The GSEs are exempt from paying state and local income taxes as well as property taxes on their offices. In a recent study[33], John Cochran and Catherine England stated that in the year 2000, the GSEs saved $1.3 billion in tax exemptions, while the Congressional Budget Office (CBO), using a different methodology, estimated the number to be $939 million. The CBO more recently estimated the tax savings to be $1.864 billion in 2002.

The Cochran study showed that since the GSEs were exempt from SEC registration and disclosure requirements, Fannie and Freddie saved an additional $176 million in 2000. Under pressure from critics, the GSEs finally agreed to voluntarily comply with SEC registration and disclosure requirements like all other public companies traded on major US exchanges.

Capital requirements

GSEs also enjoy more liberal minimum capital standard requirements over commercial banks. Regulations allow Fannie Mae to operate with a minimum capital of 2.5% of its investment portfolio, or half of what large banks are required to maintain in order to be classified as well-capitalized. Fannie is only required to maintain capital of 0.45% of the MBS that it guarantees but does not hold. Fannie Mae exceeded its capital requirements in 2003 by just $ 2.9 billion against over $2 trillion worth of mortgages it guaranteed.

As the size of the GSE portfolios has grown, so has the government subsidy. The CBO estimates that the total government subsidy to the housing GSEs in 2004 amounted to approximately $23 billion[34], of which $13.6 billion was passed on to borrowers in the form of reduced rates. The CBO claims that, on average, the subsidy is approximately 41 basis points (1 basis point = 0.01%) on GSE debt and 30 basis points on mortgage-backed securities insured by the GSEs. Only a small portion of the subsidy is passed on to the home buyer. The benefits afforded the GSEs are in addition to the ones the government extends directly to home buyers, such as mortgage interest deductibility and special tax treatment on the sale of a home. By virtue of their implicit ties with the government and the consequent private market subsidized debt issued by them, the GSEs have been under scrutiny as their presence in the mortgage marketplace has increased.

Size Matters

At the end of 2003, ranked by assets, Fannie Mae and Freddie Mac were the second and fourth largest companies in the United States, with $887 billion and $722 billion in assets, respectively. Since 2003, accounting scandals uncovered first at Freddie and then at Fannie stunted their growth, but combined, the two companies still retain control over $1.4 trillion in mortgage assets and guarantee an additional $2.6 trillion in mortgages, giving them a hand in over 40% of the $9.1 trillion home mortgage market in 2005. The debt issued by Fannie and Freddie to finance the purchase of these loan assets is equivalent to nearly 40% of the national debt.

To put the companies' growth into perspective, from 1990 to 2005, US GDP doubled, the mortgage market tripled, Fannie's and Freddie's guarantees quadrupled, and their portfolios grew ninefold, according to the Office of Federal Housing Enterprise Oversight (OFHEO). OFHEO further indicated that the notional amount of outstanding derivatives was almost $1.5 trillion for the entities versus $91 billion in 1993 when they began reporting detailed records of this statistic.

Company Risk

There is no doubt that the GSEs have been powerful and influential companies in Washington and Wall Street. Fannie and Freddie have historically been large players in the lobbying world while populating its officer, director and advisory ranks with well known Washington insiders. Along with other large corporations, the GSEs have given money to both parties to achieve their political agenda, ensuring the continuous flow of benefits to them. The GSEs' influence carries over to Wall Street as well, considering their status as two of the largest issuers of securities, awarding millions of dollars in fees to investment banks. These considerations may have complicated past efforts to reform the companies and resolve the risks associated with them.

There are some obvious and some less obvious risks assumed by Fannie and Freddie in the way they conduct their businesses. One of the obvious risks is their lack of diversification. Through no fault of their own, they were formed to help maintain liquidity in the residential mortgage market. There are restrictions as to the types of investment activities in which they can participate. When residential real estate prices tend to perform well – as they generally have since

WWII – business activity for the companies is good and default rates are low, resulting in strong growth. Additionally, business activity and default rates are favorably influenced when 10-year treasury yields, which guide most fixed mortgage rates, are stable or gradually moving lower. A prolonged period of declining interest rates has been the general experience, with a few notable exceptions since the mid-1980s. For over 20 years, the GSEs have benefited from favorable trends in demographics, household wealth, governmental policies, interest rates, money supply and economic activity. However, trend reversals can lead to lower affordability for home buyers and rising default rates, resulting in damage to the GSEs' balance sheets and income statements.

Another obvious risk assumed by the GSEs is credit risk. Credit risk is the possibility borrowers, in this case mortgage borrowers, will default on their obligations. Remember, not only do the GSEs assume the risks associated with mortgage bonds they choose to hold in their own portfolios, but they also assume the credit risk on the trillions of dollars worth of mortgages others hold, which the GSEs insure against default. Therefore, the GSEs are not only impacted by defaults on the large amounts of loans in their own portfolios, but also the loans held by other investors, which they insure. Fannie and Freddie held or insured a combined $5 trillion worth of mortgage loans that were sitting atop a capital base of $78 billion at the beginning of 2006. If defaults over the amount already reserved resulted in a 4% elimination of principal loan value for mortgages held or insured by each company, the companies could become technically insolvent.

Another obvious risk assumed by the GSEs is interest rate risk. Interest rate movements impact the GSEs in multiple ways. It impacts the level of pricing and activity in the home buying market, which can influence the default rate. Also, interest rate movements directly impact the portfolio value itself as higher rates make existing mortgage bonds less valuable. In other words, if general interest rates were to increase, existing bonds with lower fixed rates would be less attractive and therefore, would decline in price. Unlike the case with credit risk, the GSEs are only responsible for the impact fluctuating interest rates have on its own portfolio, not the securities it insures, which are held by others. For this reason, the capital requirement is less for loans the GSEs only insure.

To understand the less obvious risks assumed by the GSEs, consider the characteristics of a conventional, fixed-rate loan. Unlike most business loans, a mortgage borrower pays a fixed rate and is not penalized if he chooses to refinance his loan at any time. Since most loans last for many years, the borrower has the advantage of refinancing the mortgage and locking in a new lower rate without penalty. In the event a refinancing occurs, a mortgage holder (in this case the GSEs), will lose the higher yielding mortgage from his portfolio and is forced to reinvest the proceeds at the lower market rates. Since the entity has issued its own debt at higher interest rates, it may begin to rapidly lose money as it loses higher yielding assets (loans) from its portfolio, but continues to pay higher rates on the debt it issued.

One method of reducing this risk is for the entity holding the mortgage to match the characteristics of its liabilities with those of its assets. In other words, the entity can issue debt that is callable at any time, just like the mortgages which it holds are callable at any time. Liability matching can be more difficult in practice, however, in that investors generally do not want to hold securities that can be called away from them at the discretion of the issuer. So a mortgage bond is somewhat unique in that a buyer of the paper will be stuck with the lower coupon rate if market interest rates move higher, but will have the bond taken away from him at a previously set price if interest rates move lower. The price behavior of this type of bond is somewhat complex when plotted on a graph, with the axes being price and yield. These mortgages display what is known as negative convexity. When interest rates fall, MBS prices rise slowly; when interest rates rise, MBS prices fall quickly.

Also, the expected duration of the loan will lengthen as interest rates rise and the duration will shorten as interest rates decline. A typical non-callable bond, by contrast, pays a set interest rate for a set time period, regardless of how market interest rates behave. The price of a non-callable bond during the period between the time it is first issued and the time it matures will fluctuate. However, it will be priced at 100% of par value at the maturity date that was originally established when the bond was first issued. Alternatively, mortgage bonds will lengthen and shorten in their expected maturity during the course of their existence.

To help hedge against these risks, the GSEs make use of derivatives. The risks associated with derivatives will be discussed in greater detail in the next chapter, but one risk that should be mentioned now pertains to the vast size of the mortgage pool needed to be hedged by the GSEs. As previously indicated, the GSE holdings represent a very large proportion of the very large MBS market. Such vast amounts of risk must be hedged by creating massive notional value of derivatives with willing and able counterparties. Adding to the complexity, the nature of the risk can change as various inputs change. Extreme interest rate moves in condensed time periods can result in shifts in strategy as probabilities for default rates or duration extensions change. The GSEs and their derivative counterparties must all scramble to protect their positions in volatile times. If counterparties or other market participants step away from the market during this process, the result could be panic and dislocation in the markets.

OFHEO's Investigation

The Office of Federal Housing Enterprise and Oversight (OFHEO) regulates Fannie Mae and Freddie Mac. It was established in 1992 to ensure the capital adequacy and financial safety and soundness of the two GSEs. The agency has been chronically underfunded and understaffed considering the enormity of its appointed task. In 2002, OFHEO operated on a $30 million budget and just over 100 employees while overseeing two GSEs involved in trillions of dollars of MBSs and transactions in the 100s of billions of dollars per year.

OFHEO's relationship with Fannie Mae went through a period of acrimony when former officers of Fannie Mae and their congressional allies bitterly criticized OFHEO's then chief, Armando Falcone, in congressional hearings. The relationship between a company and its regulator is normally cooperative and professional. Although a company may have disagreements with its regulator, it would be counterproductive to publicly lambast a regulator. Aside from drawing negative attention to itself with such behavior, a company also risks alienating the regulator, resulting in harsher treatment in future interactions.

In an investigation of Fannie Mae, OFHEO cited a number of findings including Fannie Mae's senior management's interference with OFHEO's special examination. The OFHEO report, initiated in 2004 and released in 2006, also brought to light several risks posed by the GSEs. The following is the summary of the allegations contained in the 340 page "Report of the Special Examination of Fannie Mae" released in May of 2006:

> *Fannie Mae senior management promoted an image of the Enterprise (Fannie Mae) as one of the lowest-risk financial institutions in the world and as "best in class" in terms of risk management, financial*

reporting, internal control, and corporate governance. The findings in this report show that risks at Fannie Mae were greatly understated and that the image was false.

During the period covered by this report – 1998 to mid-2004 – Fannie Mae reported extremely smooth profit growth and hit announced targets for earnings per share precisely each quarter. Those achievements were illusions deliberately and systematically created by the Enterprise's senior management with the aid of inappropriate accounting and improper earnings management.

A large number of Fannie Mae's accounting policies and practices did not comply with Generally Accepted Accounting Principles (GAAP). The Enterprise also had serious problems of internal control, financial reporting, and corporate governance. Those errors resulted in Fannie Mae overstating reported income and capital by a currently estimated $10.6 billion.

By deliberately and intentionally manipulating accounting to hit earnings targets, senior management maximized the bonuses and other executive compensation they received, at the expense of shareholders. Earnings management made a significant contribution to the compensation of Fannie Mae Chairman and CEO Franklin Raines, which totaled over $90 million from 1998 to 2003. Of that total, over $52 million was directly tied to achieving earnings per share targets.

Fannie Mae consistently took a significant amount of interest rate risk and, when interest rates fell in 2002 incurred billions of dollars in economic losses. The Enterprise also had large operational and reputational risk exposures.

Fannie Mae's Board of Directors contributed to those problems by failing to be sufficiently informed and to act independently of its chairman, Franklin Raines, and other senior executives; by failing to exercise the requisite oversight over the Enterprise's operations; and by failing to discover or ensure the correction of a wide variety of unsafe and unsound practices.

The Board's failures continued in the wake of revelations of accounting problems and improper earnings management at Freddie Mac and other high profile firms, the initiation of OFHEO's special examination and credible allegations of improper earnings management made by an employee of the Enterprise's Office of the Controller.

Senior management did not make investments in accounting systems, computer systems, other infrastructure, and staffing needed to support a sound internal control system, proper accounting, and GAAP-consistent financial reporting. Those failures came at a time when Fannie Mae faced many operational challenges related to its rapid growth and changing accounting and legal requirements.

Fannie Mae senior management sought to interfere with OFHEO's special examination by directing the Enterprise's lobbyists to use their ties to Congressional staff to 1) generate a Congressional request for the Inspector General of the Department of Housing and Urban Development (HUD) to investigate OFHEO's conduct of that examination and 2) insert into an appropriations bill language that would reduce the agency's appropriations until the Director of OFHEO was replaced.

OFHEO has directed and will continue to direct Fannie Mae to take remedial actions to enhance the safe and sound operation of the Enterprise going forward. OFHEO staff recommends actions to enhance the goal of maintaining the safety and soundness of Fannie Mae.[35]

Following this and a prior report, certain recommendations were made by OFHEO and accepted by the Board of Directors of Fannie Mae. The recommendations addressed the areas of accounting practices, internal controls, governance, capital plans, corporate culture, disclosure, personnel oversight, compensation and oversight of certain corporate activities. The CEO and CFO of Fannie Mae resigned, and the auditor, KPMG, was fired. The SEC declared that Fannie Mae would have to restate prior years' earnings. The amount of the restatement is expected to be approximately $10 billion. The company further agreed to a $400 million civil penalty with OFHEO and the SEC. A class action suit was also filed by investors, charging securities fraud against the company. A two-year Department of Justice probe of criminal activity at Fannie Mae was discontinued without plans to file charges against the company, although certain individuals may still be indicted.

As of the time of this writing, the final audit needed for restatement of past earnings is ongoing but is expected to be completed by late 2006. Although changes at the company such as increased capital requirements have eased some of the risk, there is still much risk that remains.

Systemic Risk Posed By the GSEs

The size and leverage inherent in the GSEs dwarf that of LTCM, which nearly seized up the financial markets in 1998. A great deal of danger would be posed if the previously discussed risks were to cause one of the GSEs to default on its debt. Shockwaves would quickly wash over the global financial markets. The government lacking receivership powers and the GSEs lacking government guarantees could complicate an orderly government intervention. Any delay would cause prices of MBS and GSE debt to drop precipitously, which in turn could cause the markets to panic. As banks are permitted to buy GSE securities without restriction (as opposed to a cap of 10% of capital for corporate issues) the result is that more than 50% of banks hold over half of their capital in GSE debt[36]. Therefore, if an adverse event should befall GSE debt, the problem would quickly spread to the nation's banking system.

US government bond funds and money market funds also contain large holdings of GSE debt. Additionally, the derivatives market could quickly lose confidence and liquidity. The impact could also affect home buyers seeking mortgages, as investor avoidance of MBSs would lead to higher mortgage rate spreads over Treasuries, resulting in higher financing costs for new borrowers and those wishing to refinance.

If a GSE gets into financial trouble and we assume a restoration of confidence and order by the government through a successful intervention, other unintended consequences are introduced. If the government decided it would bear the losses resulting from mortgage defaults and adverse movements in interest rates, the budget deficit and national debt would be directly impacted. Money creation needed to re-liquify the system could result in inflation and a plunging dollar. Also, wrong-headed business decisions would once again be rewarded with a government backstop, further emboldening risk takers in their future expeditions.

Washington's Attempts to Rein in the GSEs

For many years the chairmen of the Subcommittee on Capital Markets, Rep. Richard Baker, (R-La), and Senate Banking Chairman Richard Shelby, (R-Ala), with the backing of the White House, have attempted to clamp down on the GSEs with substantive legislation. Their attempts have been thwarted by those siding with the GSEs from both sides of the aisle. Numerous comments have been made by Federal

Reserve Chairmen, Alan Greenspan and Ben Bernanke, as well as other financial experts without ties to the companies, as to the dangers the GSEs pose to the financial system. Despite these comments, and years after scandals were first uncovered at the housing GSEs, legislation continues to appear unlikely for the balance of 2006. Those wishing to rein in the GSEs have proposed several changes to the way in which the GSEs are regulated. The following features were found in various legislative proposals aimed at Fannie Mae and Freddie Mac:

- The reduction or elimination of the line of credit with the US treasury
- The repeal of state and local tax exemption
- The establishment of limitations on bank holdings of GSE debt
- The prohibition of political contributions by the GSEs
- Limits on lobbying activities on the part of the GSEs
- Mandatory rather than voluntary SEC registration
- The limitation or prohibition of "golden parachutes" for company executives
- The prohibition of indemnification of officers or directors
- Funding the regulator outside the appropriations process
- The formation of a new regulator with the following powers:
  - Receivership powers
  - Ability to demand a recapitalization, restructure, or liquidation of a GSE
  - Ability to demand an increase in the minimum capital requirement
  - Ability to restrict activities outside the mortgage market
  - Ability to control the GSEs' growth rate

Many would argue that the GSEs can never be regulated effectively and should be completely and unambiguously privatized. Are the advantages the GSEs bring to the system worth the risks they introduce? If we simply observe the difference in cost between a conventional GSE-backed mortgage and a non-backed jumbo mortgage, the agency backing represents a difference of approximately 0.25%. Several independent studies also point to an approximate 0.25% advantage for the home buyer. Alan Greenspan in comments to Congress declared the benefit provided by the GSEs was "between de minimus and small"[37]. Why then should government benefits, perceived or real, be extended to enterprises that consume a large part of the benefit for its officers and shareholders while endangering the financial system? An arrangement has been established where profits are privatized (awarded to the companies) and risks socialized (borne by tax payers).

Some may counter that even a quarter point savings for a marginal home buyer could play a meaningful part in the decision to buy a home. However, a "subsidized" interest rate can quickly result in higher prices in homes, dissipating much of the subsidy. In other words, if all else is equal, builders and existing home sellers will demand higher prices if interest rates are lower. Trying to improve upon the free market solution does not work. The law of supply and demand should be allowed to dictate the cost of a home as well as the cost of the loan to purchase the home.

Chapter 4

A Leveraged System & Its Players

Leverage

Leverage refers to the use of financial instruments or borrowed capital, such as margin, to increase the potential return of an investment. Leverage allows the investor to take a position which is more than the amount that the investor could own by paying for it in full. For example, when trading stocks on margin, the investor is required to put up a margin deposit, which may be as little as 50% of the transaction. Thus, an investor may purchase 100 shares of a $100 per share stock for as little as $5,000 in payment and $5,000 borrowed. If the stock rises 10% ($110/share), the next day he can sell the stock and realize a profit of $1,000 on his $5,000 outlay. He realizes a gain of 20% (disregarding the interest owed on the margin loan), or twice the percentage gain in the stock price. Of course, the math works in reverse if the stock declines. If the stock becomes worthless, not only does the investor lose the $5,000 he deposited, but an additional $5,000 he must repay for the margin loan.

Margin is a simple example of the use of leverage. Certain financial instruments can represent much greater multiples of underlying securities. Leverage is a double-edged sword; while it allows an investor to make more money with a smaller amount of capital, it can also result in larger losses if the investor is on the wrong side of a price move.

Derivatives

"Perhaps the clearest evidence of the perceived benefits that derivatives have provided is their continued spectacular growth."
– Federal Reserve Chairman Alan Greenspan at the Federal Reserve Bank of Chicago's 41st Annual Conference on Bank Structure, Chicago, Illinois, May 5, 2005

A derivative is a financial instrument whose value is dependent on the value of another underlying asset. The underlying asset can be a financial security, commodity, index or event. An option is an example of a derivative. The value of an option is dependent on the value of the underlying asset, but it can offer greater percentage movements and require less out-of-pocket money than an outright purchase of the underlying asset.

Derivatives originated quite early in history. Derivative contracts have been found written on clay tablets from Mesopotamia, dating back to 1750 BC. Aristotle mentioned an option on the use of olive oil presses in his *Politics* about 2,500 years ago. The Japanese traded futures-like contracts on warehouse receipts for rice in the 1700s. In the US, forward and futures contracts have been traded on the Chicago Board of Trade since 1849. Over the years, mathematicians and financiers struggled to become proficient at assigning proper values to these contracts. In 1973, Myron Scholes and Fischer Black introduced their famous Black-Scholes Option Pricing Model. This mathematical model takes into account a security's current price, its implied volatility, strike price, time until expiration, risk free rate of return, and the standard deviation of the security's return generating a theoretical value for the derivative. The 1980s saw a rapid expansion of derivatives, perhaps due to the volatility of exchange rates, interest rates and inflation prevalent during the 1970s and 1980s. The increased volatility prompted clients in the financial sector to seek instruments that would help in managing the risks. Thus, derivatives were used as hedging instruments that allowed users to manage risk at a relatively low cost.

Derivatives can either be listed through an exchange or privately traded between two parties over-the-counter. The ones that are listed on an exchange are subject to greater regulation and tend to be more standardized than those that are transacted over-the-counter. Derivatives are measured by their notional value, which is the market value of the amount of underlying asset that a particular derivative controls. At year-end 2005, the notional value of global over-the-counter derivatives was estimated by the Bank of International Settlements (BIS) to exceed $284 trillion. The total notional amount of exchange traded derivatives stood at $58 trillion for a total of $342 trillion[38], or to express it another way, one-third of $1 quadrillion. The gross market value for all derivatives – which is a better measure of global systemic risk exposure – is closer to $10 trillion, still a staggering sum when compared to a total global GDP of just over $40 trillion. By using these instruments, various risks have been efficiently transferred to institutions with different objectives or tolerances for risk. The growing use of derivatives has also led to heightened competition in the financial sector, prompting its creators to come out with new and increasingly complex derivatives.

Various Types of Derivatives

Although there are many variations of asset-based derivatives, those commonly traded relate to interest rate risk, credit risk, currency risk or price risk. Figures released by the International Swaps and Derivatives Association[39] show that 80% of the world's top 500 companies utilize interest rate derivatives to manage their cash flow. Approximately 75% use foreign exchange contracts, 25% use commodity contracts and 10% use equity options.

Interest rate derivatives allow for the hedging or speculation of changes in interest rates. This segment comprises the largest derivatives market in the world. About $215 trillion of the total $342 trillion in derivatives consist of interest rate contracts in one form or another. Credit derivatives allow for the hedging or speculating in the default or credit downgrade of an underlying security. The credit default market has experienced tremendous growth over the last several years.

In the following section, we look at the different classes of derivatives and some of the more commonly traded derivative types.

Forward Contracts

In a forward contract, two parties agree to buy or sell any asset at an agreed upon price at a specified point in the future. They are neither standardized nor traded on an exchange; they are transacted privately. For example, if Party A needs to buy foreign currency at a specified point in the future, he is exposed to currency risk due to the fact the price of the foreign currency may be higher when he requires it. To hedge this risk, A can enter into a forward contract with Party B, who would agree to provide A with the foreign currency at a price that is fixed at today's level. Thus, party A transfers the currency risk to which he is exposed to party B.

The forward price of such a contract is commonly contrasted with the spot price, which is the current price at which the asset changes hands in the open market. The difference between the spot and the forward price is the forward premium or discount. A forward contract is useful for those wanting to customize their hedge or speculative position.

A **forward rate agreement** (FRA) is a type of forward contract in which two parties agree to an interest rate on a debt obligation beginning on a specified future date. The payments are calculated over a notional amount for a predefined period and netted, i.e., only the difference between the beginning price and ending price is paid. This amount is paid on the termination date.

The sale and simultaneous agreement to repurchase certain securities at a specified time and price is known as a **repurchase agreement** (repo). Repos have been traditionally used by banks as a source or use of short-term funds, often overnight. The market, however, has proliferated to the extent that hedge funds and other market participants frequently use the repo market as a funding device. For example, if a hedge fund trades a Treasury bond option and hedges it with the purchase of the underlying treasury bonds, the hedger can then enter into a repurchase agreement to fund the bond purchase. A **reverse repo** is the mirror image of a repo. It is the purchase and simultaneous agreement to sell back certain securities at a specified time and price.

Futures Contracts

As we have discussed, a forward contract is an agreement between two parties who negotiate among themselves. An inherent problem with forwards is finding the appropriate parties to agree to various parameters. A standardized forward contract that is traded on an exchange is called a futures contract. Futures contracts are standardized as to date, quantity, quality and delivery specifications of the underlying asset.

The most common futures exchanges are the Chicago Board of Trade, the Chicago Mercantile Exchange, the Kansas City Board of Trade and the New York Mercantile Exchange. Futures are traded on financial assets (stocks, bonds, currencies, etc.) and commodities (grains, livestock, metals, energy, etc.). More exotic futures contracts have appeared in recent years, such as pollution control credits and weather futures. The firms and individuals that deal in futures with the public are required to register and are subject to regulation by the Commodity Futures Trading Commission (CFTC) and the National Futures Association (NFA). The exchanges themselves are also regulated by the CFTC. However, these rules and regulations do not apply to over-the-counter derivatives which are not traded on an exchange.

Swaps

A swap is an agreement to trade the netted-out value of two series of payments, oftentimes between an underlying security with fixed payments versus one with variable payments. But swaps can be performed to exchange two fixed-rate cash flows, particularly if the flows are irregular.

Interest rate swaps are the most commonly used derivatives, with $172 trillion in notional value at the end of 2005. Interest rate swaps are commonly used by companies to reallocate their exposure to interest rate variations, usually by exchanging fixed rate obligations for floating rate obligations.

The **credit default swap** or CDS has become the engine of the credit derivatives market, offering liquid price discovery, sometimes trading with higher volumes than the underlying asset (bond) itself. A CDS is an agreement between a protection buyer (the insured) and a protection seller (the insurer), whereby the buyer pays a periodic fee in return for a contingent payment by the seller upon an adverse credit event happening in the reference entity. A CDS is similar to the agreement between a homeowner and an insurance company. The contingent payment made by the insurer usually replicates the loss incurred by the holder of the reference entity's debt in the event of default. It covers only the credit risk embedded in the asset. Risks arising from other factors, such as interest rate movements, remain with the buyer.

For example, a fund that owns ABC bonds may wish to protect

itself against a bankruptcy filing. In order to do so, the fund manager purchases a CDS, whereby the fund pays a specified amount to the seller of a CDS in return for a payment in the event that ABC files for bankruptcy within the specified time period. Banks, brokerage firms and hedge funds were net buyers of protection, whereas insurance companies were net sellers of protection. In particular, monoline insurers specializing in only credit insurance carried a large portion of the credit risk in 2004.

Synthetic **collateralized debt obligations** (CDOs) are credit derivatives offering diversification through exposure to a large number of companies in a single instrument. CDO exposure is sold in slices of varying risk or subordination – each slice is known as a tranche. In a cash-flow CDO, the intrinsic credit risks are the risks associated with the bonds/loans held in the CDO. Alternatively, in a synthetic CDO, the risks are represented by underlying credit derivatives such as credit default swaps rather than the physical bonds or loans.

OTC Options

An over-the-counter (OTC) option refers to a type of derivative that gives the holder a right (but not an obligation) to purchase or sell a security within a predetermined time in the future, for a predefined amount. The seller of the option has the obligation to honor the contract as per the discretion of the buyer. Since an option contract grants the buyer a right, but not an obligation, the buyer has something of value. In exchange for this value, the buyer pays the seller an option premium. OTC options are negotiated and traded privately between parties.

An **interest rate cap** is a commonly used option that ensures that the purchaser's rate of interest is capped at a maximum rate, whereas an **interest rate floor** ensures the rate will not fall below a specified level.

A **swaption** is a swap and option hybrid which grants the owner an option to enter an interest rate swap in the future. A swap, as discussed earlier, is a contract in which the parties will exchange the cash flows associated with the items they are swapping. The party buying the swaption may not want to actually carry out the swap unless some market condition is reached, in which case he can exercise the option to enter into the swap.

Players in the Derivatives Market

Commercial banks, securities houses, hedge funds, insurance companies, mutual funds and pension funds are the main participants in derivatives trading. They can act as hedgers seeking to mitigate risk or speculators seeking to earn good returns in exchange for the assumed risk. Arbitrageurs, on the other hand, try to exploit perceived imbalanced pricing between two or more identical or correlated financial instruments on different markets or in different forms.

Risks and Rewards Associated with Derivatives

> *"Derivatives are financial weapons of mass destruction."*
> – Warren Buffett

The growth in derivatives has served to lubricate the wheels of finance and has contributed greatly to the growth in GDP and a better standard of living for the general population. In its genesis thousands of years ago, derivatives contributed to the growth in commercial agriculture and presently help to facilitate growth in a variety of industries. In comments before the Committee on Banking and Financial Services in July of 1998, Alan Greenspan indicated that the huge growth in the derivatives market reflects the judgement of the participants that these instruments provide protection against undue asset concentration risk and are clearly perceived to add significant value to our financial structure. He went on to add that "inappropriate regulation distorts the efficiency of our market system and as a consequence impedes growth and improvement in standards of living."[40]

Derivatives are distinctly more complex than traditional financial securities. In previous sections, we have discussed the evolution of the derivatives market, the types of derivatives available and the players in the market. The discussion indicated how risk can be reduced by shifting these risks to investors who are paid to assume risk. However, the derivatives market has perils that must be considered in light of its sheer size and its importance to our economy.

An important distinction must be made between risks associated with various entities, market instruments, and strategies versus systemic risks. The derivatives marketplace poses risks to those who participate in it, yet most have done a reasonably good job of neutralizing many of those risks. Occasional losses are an inevitable consequence when trading in the financial markets. Losses can grow larger and more rapidly when leverage is utilized, leading to occasional insolvencies among participants that can potentially lead to contagion effects.

We can identify some of the gaps in risk analysis, and then discuss their potential to impact our financial system and the economy at large. Risks of leverage and a lack of understanding can be illustrated by case studies of Orange County, Gibson Greetings and Procter & Gamble.

Orange County Case

In December 1994, the municipality of Orange County, California, shocked markets when it announced that its investment pool had suffered a staggering loss of $1.6 billion, the largest ever recorded by a local government investment pool, causing the county to go bankrupt. The loss was the result of risky investments made by the County Treasurer who was entrusted with a $7.5 billion portfolio belonging to county schools, cities, special districts and the county itself. Using its holding of securities as collateral, through leverage and derivatives, primarily reverse repos, it built up a position of over $20.5 billion on its $7.5 billion equity base. The aim was to increase the county's income by taking advantage of the higher yields given by medium-term maturities when compared to short-term investments. For example, in December 1993, short-term yields were just shy of 3%, but 5-year yields on GSE-issue notes were close to 5.2%.

Cash flowed into the portfolio through a combination of borrowing at lower short-term rates and lending at higher intermediate-term rates – thereby capturing a spread between the yields – and leveraging this through the use of reverse repos and structured notes. In effect, profits were dependent on interest rates staying low and yield spreads staying wide. However, that did not happen. In February 1994, the Federal Reserve initiated a series of six consecutive hikes in interest rates and the price of bonds in the Orange County portfolio declined in value. The county was thus left with a leveraged portfolio of diminishing value and higher borrowing costs, resulting in large losses which led to its bankruptcy filing.

Gibson Greetings Case

In this case, derivatives used were linked to interest rate movements. From November 1991 to March 1994, bankers sold Gibson approximately 29 derivatives transactions. Over time, these derivatives became increasingly complex, risky and intertwined. Many of them possessed leverage factors that spectacularly increased Gibson's losses even though the changes in interest rates were relatively small.

Gibson was sold customized securities that were not traded in the open market. Consequently, its bankers used sophisticated computer models to ascertain values for these customized derivatives. Since Gibson had no expertise or its own computer models to value these derivatives, it ended up using the information provided by its bankers regarding the value of its derivatives positions in order to evaluate particular transactions and to prepare its financial statements.

Gibson's bankers allegedly gave misleading information regarding the actual position of the derivatives. When the real position was revealed, Gibson found itself with a loss of over $20 million.

Proctor & Gamble Case

In the case of Proctor & Gamble, the derivatives the company used were interest rate swaps, along with foreign exchange swaps. In 1995, P&G lost $157 million on these derivatives, mostly due to an inadequate understanding of the risks associated with the products. Despite its size, P&G apparently lacked the sophistication to analyze the derivatives it was using, claiming the terms and risks were not adequately discussed. Although this case occurred several years ago, it illustrates how the derivatives market can be murky.

As these case studies show, derivatives are complex products which, if not understood properly, can lead to an increase in risks rather than a reduction in them. Although decision makers have become more sophisticated in their understanding of derivatives, much of the derivatives market has become more complex. Assuming we get beyond the risk of a lack of understanding on the part of derivative players, there are other more significant risks associated with derivatives that can impose great danger on the financial system. These risks are discussed below.

Counterparty/Credit Risk

The risk arising from the possibility of derivatives issuing firms defaulting on their derivative obligations is known as counterparty risk. Any agreement involving two counterparties involves such risks.

For example, OTC option holders must acknowledge the possibility of the option writer defaulting on the payoff amount. Any player in the derivatives market must take into account the risk that the other party will not make good on its obligation. The entity that purchases the derivative is the one that bears the risk of the counterparty performing on its obligation. A sophisticated derivatives buyer may demand a discount for a given derivative purchase from a counterparty that is not as financially sound as another issuer.

Certain financial institutions require specific standards of counterparties prior to entering into transactions with them. However, many do not have strict standards and this opens the door to abuse. For example, a thinly capitalized institution can write large amounts of credit insurance for another financial company which holds bonds in Acme Corporation. The writer or insurer might be issuing more insurance than it could cover should Acme file for bankruptcy. The institution holding Acme bonds operates under the belief that its position is hedged. If the derivative counterparty does not make good on its contract in the event of Acme's bankruptcy filing, and the value of its bonds falls, the institution would be left with large unanticipated losses.

Even a well capitalized diversified entity writing default insurance can become insolvent if it has written too much insurance when an adverse event befalls a particular industry to which it has significant exposure, or if an event impacts the markets as a whole. Typical insurance tends to insure random and independent risks. Given a large enough population, insurance companies are fairly accurate at predicting how many deaths, house fires or automobile accidents will occur in a given year. A house fire in one neighborhood generally does not increase the likelihood of a fire in another neighborhood. Also, the cause of a fire in New York generally does not cause another fire in Florida, they tend to be random and independent events. Predictability allows insurance companies to reserve a small amount of capital in relation to the overall potential risk. If in a given year, an insurance company experiences a 20% accident rate for automobiles it insures, it would most likely become insolvent.

The writers of credit and other types of risk are subject to risks that are neither random nor independent. If a severe recession quickly strikes the economy, many marginal companies in different industries will be impacted. Also, a number of bankruptcy filings can lead to additional problems for entities that rely on those companies for their own business survival. A writer of credit insurance can quickly find out in such an environment that diversification will provide little relief.

Liquidity Risk/Herd Risk

Liquidity risk arises when much of the market may be interested in a similar kind of protection at the same time. For instance, assume that a large part of the market anticipates a general increase in interest rates. Utilizing various methods, market participants establish hedges to protect against a rise in rates. Writers of this insurance oftentimes utilize their own strategies to cover potential losses, such as dynamic delta hedging.

Delta is the change in price of an option for every one point move in the underlying security. To remain properly hedged, the insurer may buy or sell derivatives of the underlying bond as time goes by, to hedge against the further adverse movement of the bond. If a large number of players deploy this strategy, then it can directly impact the actual movement of the underlying security. If this self-reinforcing activity or another outside influence causes a large rapid move, it may lead to a position not being properly hedged, resulting in large leveraged losses.

Large rapid price movements can, in turn, lead to widening bid/offer spreads and diminished liquidity, further aggravating losses and leading to a potential melt down. Computer models tend to reflect probabilities, but not absolute truths. It is when conditions are out of whack that low probability events can occur.

Operational Risk

Effective management of legal, custody and systems issues is an important component of proper derivative portfolio management. So too are diligent and competent management of such complex instruments. Operational risks can arise when systems are not properly set up to assess changes in risk as the underlying value of the derivative changes in price. It can also relate to lack of sufficient information on the risk characteristics of the derivative product.

As more participants and more capital enter an already colossal derivatives market, the risks described previously can exert immense pressure on the entire financial system. Lacking sufficient oversight and transparency, new inexperienced fringe participants can initiate a chain reaction, with devastating consequences.

Warnings from a Market Guru

The following was extracted from the 2005 Chairman's letter to shareholders of Berkshire Hathaway, dated February 28th 2006. Chairman Warren Buffett detailed the difficulty he and his right hand man, Charlie Munger, had in closing down the derivative book which Berkshire inherited through its acquisition of General Re.

> ...We lost $104 million pre-tax last year in our continuing attempt to exit Gen Re's derivative operation. Our aggregate losses since we began this endeavor total $404 million.
>
> Originally we had 23,218 contracts outstanding. By the start of 2005 we were down to 2,890. You might expect that our losses would have been stemmed by this point, but the blood has kept flowing. Reducing our inventory to 741 contracts last year cost us the $104 million mentioned above.
>
> Remember that the rationale for establishing this unit in 1990 was Gen Re's wish to meet the needs of insurance clients. Yet one of the contracts we liquidated in 2005 had a term of 100 years! It's difficult to imagine what "need" such a contract could fulfill except, perhaps, the need of a compensation-conscious trader to have a long-dated contract on his books. Long contracts, or alternatively those with multiple variables, are the most difficult to mark to market (the standard procedure used in accounting for derivatives) and provide the most opportunity for "imagination" when traders are estimating their value. Small wonder that traders promote them.
>
> A business in which huge amounts of compensation flow from assumed numbers is obviously fraught with danger. When two traders execute a transaction that has several, sometimes esoteric, variables and a far-off settlement date, their respective firms must subsequently value these contracts whenever they calculate their earnings. A given contract may be valued at one price by Firm A and at another by Firm B. You can bet that the valuation differences – and I'm personally familiar with several that were huge – tend to be tilted in a direction favoring higher earnings at each firm. It's a strange world in which two parties can carry out a paper transaction that each can promptly report as profitable.
>
> ...I wasted several years while we attempted to sell the operation. That was a doomed endeavor because no realistic solution could have extricated us from the maze of liabilities that was going to exist for

decades. Our obligations were particularly worrisome because their potential to explode could not be measured. Moreover, if severe trouble occurred, we knew it was likely to correlate with problems elsewhere in financial markets.

...The second reason I regularly describe our problems in this area lies in the hope that our experiences may prove instructive for managers, auditors and regulators. In a sense, we are a canary in this business coal mine and should sing a song of warning as we expire. The number and value of derivative contracts outstanding in the world continues to mushroom and is now a multiple of what existed in 1998, the last time that financial chaos erupted.

Our experience should be particularly sobering because we were a better-than-average candidate to exit gracefully. Gen Re was a relatively minor operator in the derivatives field. It has had the good fortune to unwind its supposedly liquid positions in a benign market, all the while free of financial or other pressures that might have forced it to conduct the liquidation in a less-than-efficient manner. Our accounting in the past was conventional and actually thought to be conservative. Additionally, we know of no bad behavior by anyone involved.

It could be a different story for others in the future. Imagine, if you will, one or more firms (troubles often spread) with positions that are many multiples of ours attempting to liquidate in chaotic markets and under extreme, and well-publicized pressures. This is a scenario to which much attention should be given now rather than after the fact. The time to have considered – and improved – the reliability of New Orleans' levees was before Katrina.

When we finally wind up Gen Re Securities, my feelings about its departure will be akin to those expressed in a country song, "My wife ran away with my best friend, and I sure miss him a lot."[41]

Hedge Funds

A hedge fund is an investment company with less regulation and greater flexibility than mutual funds. Many of the rules and regulations governing mutual funds do not apply to hedge funds and this allows them to seek higher returns while accepting higher risk. Many hedge funds are restricted by law to a maximum of 100 investors per fund, which is why most hedge funds set very high minimum investment amounts, usually starting at $250,000 and going to over $1 million. Hedge funds also enjoy greater flexibility in devising their fee structures.

A.W. Jones, in 1949, created what is considered to be the first hedge fund in the United States. One part of his investment portfolio consisted of shares that would increase if the market rose. Another part consisted of short positions that would benefit him if the market fell. His fund was therefore hedged and the term 'hedge fund' emerged.

Hedge fund strategies, as we shall see, have now become a lot more complicated. In the 1960s, as Jones's fund continued to do well, it received more publicity, which encouraged more hedge funds to enter the market. In 2006, there were more than 7,000 hedge funds around the world, managing more than $1.3 trillion of investments compared to fewer than 600 funds managing $40 billion in 1990. One thing that makes them attractive for investors is the fact that even in a low-return investment environment they still offer the hope of double-digit annual returns. Wall Street also benefits from the hedge funds, by earning a large portion of its total revenue from hedge funds' trading commissions.

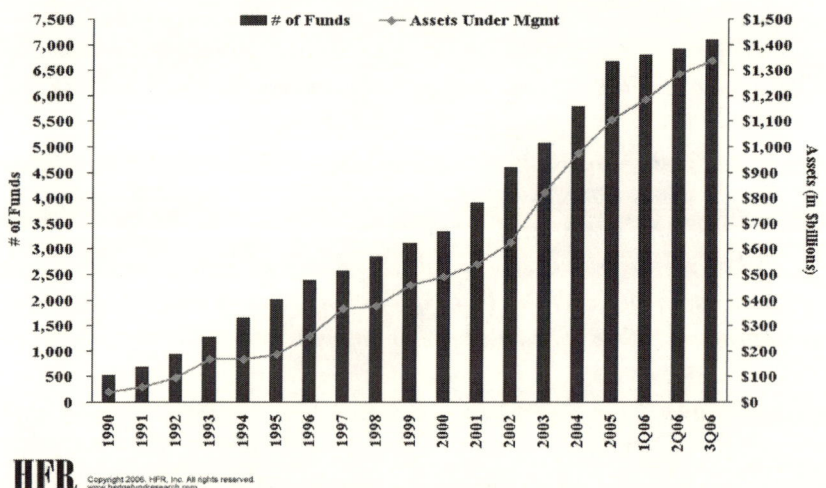

Source: Hedge Fund Research (HFR) www.hedgefundresearch.com and Citigroup

Differences between Mutual Funds and Hedge Funds

While a hedge fund and a mutual fund both have fund managers managing investors' money, they differ in many ways. These include the degree of regulatory scrutiny, fee structure, leveraging practices, liquidity and investor characteristics.

Regulation

Mutual funds in the US are among the most strictly regulated financial products. They are subject to numerous requirements that have been designed to ensure that they operate in the best interests of their shareholders. Hedge funds, though, are private investment pools subject to far less regulatory scrutiny.

Mutual fund companies must register with the US Securities and Exchange Commission (SEC) and every facet of their structure and operations is subject to regulation under four federal laws: the Securities Act of 1933, the Securities Exchange Act of 1934, the Investment Company Act of 1940 and the Investment Advisers Act of 1940.

The SEC oversees the mutual fund industry's compliance with these regulations. The Internal Revenue Code has additional requirements with regard to a fund's portfolio diversification and its distribution of earnings. The National Association of Securities Dealers, Inc. (NASD) acts as a watchdog over the advertisements and other sales content of mutual fund companies. In addition, mutual funds must have directors who are responsible for the fund's policies and procedures, with at least 75% of the directors and the chairman of the fund board being independent of the fund's management.

The Investment Company Act is the foundation of all mutual fund regulation. In addition to regulating the structure and operation of mutual funds and requiring funds to safeguard their portfolio securities, the Act also requires them to maintain detailed records. The 1933 Act requires all prospective investors be given a prospectus containing detailed and specific information about the mutual fund's management, its holdings, fees and other expenses, besides its performance.

Hedge funds, however, are private investment funds with terms that are agreements between the sponsors of the fund and the investors. The rapid growth of the hedge fund industry prompted the SEC to initiate a study, which in October 2004 mandated that hedge fund advisers be required to register under the Investment Advisers Act. The new rules, among other things, would have allowed the SEC to inspect the backgrounds of hedge fund advisers and to deny registration to any hedge fund adviser if he/she was found unsuitable. This included a disciplinary record or a past felony conviction. However, in June of 2006, the U.S. Court of Appeals for the District of Columbia Circuit struck down the SEC's ruling. Christopher Cox, Chairman of the SEC, said that the agency would not appeal the ruling, but would attempt to move ahead with an alternative plan the details of which were not available at the time of this writing.

Fee Structure

A mutual fund's fees and expenses are required to be disclosed in detail as a fee table in the prospectus. The sales charges and other distribution fees are also subject to limits under NASD rules. In contrast, hedge funds have much more flexibility in designing their fee structures. Usually, the hedge fund manager charges a fee of 1-2% based on the fund's assets and a performance fee of about 20% of the profits.

Leveraging Practices

The Investment Company Act of 1940 lays down the guidelines regarding the amounts that a mutual fund can borrow against the value of securities in its portfolio. SEC requirements restrict the extent of leveraging that mutual fund managers can employ. In contrast, many hedge funds thrive on leverage and high-risk strategies. Hedge fund advisers use diverse investment and trading strategies in an attempt to maximize returns.

Liquidity and Pricing

By law, mutual funds value their portfolios and disclose their net asset value (NAV) every day. Traded securities within the portfolio need to be valued at market price while unlisted, or thinly traded securities are valued at fair market value. Based on the NAV, investors can redeem their holdings on any given business day, although a back-end fee is sometimes imposed.

In contrast, rules regarding hedge fund pricing are much more lax. Hedge fund investors are not always able to determine the value of their investment at any given time. Furthermore, investors are subject to lock-in requirements, often limiting access to their capital to once a quarter or once a year. And a standardized methodology to determine valuations of illiquid derivatives is lacking. More subjective judgement is involved in portfolio valuations.

Investor Profile

To invest in a mutual fund, one needs the minimum amount, which is usually $1,000, sometimes lower. Many investors deposit small amounts over a period of years as part of their long-term investment plans. There are over 90 million, mostly middle income Americans who own mutual fund shares.

Hedge fund investors are often required to invest a minimum of $250,000. Therefore, the profile of a typical hedge fund investor is a higher net worth individual or institution. In fact, under the National Securities Markets Improvement Act of 1996, some hedge funds can only accept investments from individuals who hold at least $5 million in investments. Since hedge funds are relatively unregulated pools of investment, the goal is to restrict participation to sophisticated investors. Hedge funds can accept money from other types of investors under exemptions provided by the Investment Company Act.

Hedge Fund Strategies

There are three broadly defined hedge fund sectors, each consisting of various investment strategies.

1. **Global macro funds** seek to take advantage of broad moves in various markets or sectors. Managers tend to utilize either a fundamental or quantitative approach to determine the markets in which they wish to participate. Managers tend to specialize in equities, fixed income or futures markets.

2. **Sector/Company/Asset-specific funds** focus on company-specific or transaction-specific opportunities rather than trying to determine general market direction. The various strategy-specific managers in this category include long/short; short only, opportunistic, asset specific and distressed debt.

3. **Arbitrage funds** take advantage of discrepancies between various securities. A mergers and acquisition specialist may focus on the discrepancy between the securities of the acquirer and the acquiree.

Other specialists focus on convertible arbitrage or fixed income arbitrage.

Through the use of leverage, the industry's outright investments are larger than the $1.3 trillion in invested equity. Most hedge funds are extremely focused and rely on the specific expertise of the fund manager or the management team. Unlike regular equity or mutual funds that are usually fully exposed to market risks; the performance of many hedge funds, especially those employing relative value strategies, may not be dependent on the movements of bond or equity markets as a whole.

Moreover, many hedge fund strategies, specifically arbitrage strategies, are sometimes limited as to how much capital they can successfully deploy before returns diminish, i.e., illiquid situations where inefficient pricing has been driven out through monetary exploitation by the fund's manager. Thus, many good hedge fund managers limit the amount of capital they accept.

But hedge funds are also prone to conflicts of interest. Fund managers are paid a portion of the earnings of the portfolio. Thus, less scrupulous fund managers may try to maximize returns by taking inappropriate risks. If the fund performs poorly, the managers still make an asset-based management fee, and they are free to move to another fund if there is little hope of earning the incentive fee. If outsized bets pay off, they are rewarded handsomely. Also, a manager may inflate, intentionally or unintentionally, the valuation of illiquid securities, causing returns to appear higher than they really are.

Hedge funds usually attract highly sophisticated investors such as high net worth individuals, endowments, pension funds and banks, who understand the risks. Over time, many hedge funds have shown good relative performance and low correlations to the stock and bond markets. However, it is difficult to predict the risks that may arise from the proliferation of hedge funds. More players with more money lead to fewer investment opportunities to exploit. This can lead to the utilization of greater leverage to multiply smaller margins in order to achieve acceptable profits, but while accepting commensurately greater risks. One of the most celebrated hedge funds – Long Term Capital Management (LTCM) – demonstrated spectacular success but ultimately collapsed in dramatic fashion.

The LTCM Story

Long Term Capital Management was founded in 1994 by John Meriwether, a famous bond trader with Salomon Brothers. Meriwether put together a team of top traders and academicians, including Nobel Laureates. The objective of the fund was to use the best traders' market judgments along with quantitative modeling knowledge to generate superior returns. Thanks to its high profile team, the fund started with $1.3 billion from investors that included large investment banks and other sophisticated investors. Initially, the fund did extremely well, extracting arbitrage profits by trading in various securities. But by 1998 – in just four years – it ran up huge losses and hovered on the brink of default. The collapse of a fund the size of LTCM threatened a systemic collapse, prompting the Federal Reserve to help organize a $3.5 billion rescue package from leading American banks.

LTCM's strategy was designed to make money by extracting profits through arbitrage. Following a convergence strategy, their traders looked for securities which were mispriced relative to other similar ones, buying the undervalued ones and selling short the overvalued ones. Ultimately the prices were supposed to converge; then the positions would be closed out and profits realized. The four main types of trade were:

- Convergence among US, Japanese and European government bonds;
- Convergence among European government bonds;
- Convergence between recently issued versus seasoned US government bonds;
- Long positions in emerging markets' government bonds, hedged back to dollars.

Due to the fact the mismatch in the prices was relatively small, huge leveraged positions were needed to make meaningful profits. By 1998, LTCM's equity base had grown to $5 billion and it borrowed an additional $125 billion. The leverage factor was over 25:1. Its computer models, however, predicted that the positions it was accumulating were low risk.

Things went well until May 1998 when returns turned negative. The situation worsened in August when the Russian government defaulted on its government bonds (GKOs). LTCM had hedged its GKO positions by selling Russian rubles. It believed that if the Russian government defaulted on its payments, the currency value would also collapse. Therefore potential losses on the bonds would be offset by profits on the currency trades. Unfortunately, the banks guaranteeing the ruble hedges closed down when the ruble collapsed, and the Russian government stopped all trading in its currency.

While this was a huge setback for LTCM, it was not enough to bring down the hedge fund. But a 'flight to liquidity' occurred in fixed income markets across the world, and losses multiplied. Other fund managers began to shift into securities that were more liquid, moving from Japanese, European and emerging markets debt paper to US Treasury bonds, specifically recently-issued or 'on-the-run' Treasuries that traditionally were the most liquid of securities.

One would expect that a recently issued Treasury bond coming due on the same date as an older Treasury bond should provide the same yield. They are both fully backed by the US Treasury. However, recently issued bonds tend to trade with lower yields (higher price) because there is more activity or liquidity for a time. As time passes, it too becomes a seasoned bond and will trade at the same yield as the older bond, with the spotlight shifting to a newer 'on-the-run bond'. LTCM had exploited this discrepancy by shorting the more expensive 'on-the-run bond', waiting for it to close the gap with the older bonds which it owned. When the flight to liquidity occurred in the market, the spread between recently issued and older or 'seasoned' securities unexpectedly widened. A huge portion of LTCM's balance sheet was exposed to changes in the value of liquidity. LTCM's position, built on convergence trading, suddenly found prices diverging. By September, the fund had lost over $1.8 billion of its capital. LTCM needed more capital and tried to get additional money. However, the Federal Reserve had to help engineer a rescue package with the help of major US banks to prevent a default that would have had major repercussions for the global financial system. There are several lessons to be learned from the LTCM collapse.

1. **Don't mistake intelligence for wisdom** when evaluating portfolio managers, even those with Nobel Laureates on staff. It is extremely difficult to properly neutralize risk through the use of derivatives. LTCM in its glory days earned returns of 40% but ultimately failed to understand the risks that it was carrying, and when markets acted irrationally, the computer models turned upside down. An intellectual may consider the odds of an event to be so remote as to be negligible.

However, the tiny tail of the probability bell curve occasionally rises up to strike a devastating blow to portfolios. Unexpected events inevitably occur in our complex global economy. When these events are combined with an extremely leveraged financial system containing pricing distortions due to an over-liquefied environment, the result can be lethal. Unlikely events can lead to unlikely responses in the marketplace, resulting in massive losses.

2. **Leverage can be a double-edged sword:** LTCM depended on exploiting the deviation between market values and fair values of particular assets. It was convinced that it was only a matter of time before the fair value and the market value would converge and profits would ensue. The problem with such an approach is that it requires patience, and when markets are in crisis, patience is in short supply. In early 1998, LTCM's total investment portfolio was well over $100 billion, while its total equity was about $4 billion; its swaps position was valued at over $1 trillion notional, which was equivalent to 5% of the entire global market. Once portfolio assets begin a decline, all losses impact the equity or book value of the portfolio while the debt remains intact. While extreme leverage can provide large returns in good markets, equity can quickly disappear in bad markets.

3. **Liquidity Risk:** Most models used by LTCM – and other hedge funds – did not explicitly use liquidity risk in modeling. The securities were not classified as illiquid or very liquid. When the flight to liquidity took place, LTCM was caught off guard. Therefore, liquidity risk should be a part of modeling. Now most hedge funds include liquidity risk in their models, but it is a very difficult parameter to quantify.

4. **The need for disclosure and transparency:** LTCM, like most hedge funds, was unregulated. Thus, its fund managers could act without investors or regulators having knowledge of their activities. Dire events may not have reached such levels had there been adequate regulation and disclosure.

Systemic Risk

Considering that the OTC derivatives markets and hedge funds are largely unregulated, coupled with their rapid growth, one must assess the potential problems that can develop. We've already defined some of the risks and ordeals certain entities experienced when trying to extricate themselves from their risky endeavors. The overriding issue lies in the potential emergence of a full-blown systemic financial crisis. The probability of such a scenario is impossible to determine, but it is not zero.

A sharp decline in a particular sector or asset class that catches leveraged players on the wrong side of the trade can lead to certain predictable behaviors. When losses are sufficiently steep, investors must act to mitigate risk. This can involve outright liquidation of the declining securities, the purchase of protection against further losses, or the sale of other assets to raise liquidity. Other participants, sensing trouble and seeking profits, may enter the fray to get out in front of the risk mitigation efforts of those in trouble. Thus, higher prices for protection and declining prices for the securities in liquidation potentially lead to a negative spiral, which can be disastrous.

As prices fall below modeled levels, additional large amounts of the assets may be listed for sale causing the trades to become crowded thus drying up liquidity. Fear is a potent psychological force, and it may enter the market as concerns grow that certain participants may become insolvent. Even relatively small monoline insurance companies or hedge funds, by leverage, can be counterparties to large amounts of derivative assets. The introduction of counterparty credit risk causes traders to not only consider the expected direction of prices but also the viability of participants on the other side of their trades. Most firms perform counterparty risk analysis before commencing a business relationship with another entity, but often information on risks associated with its portfolio's positions or strategies is not disclosed, and this is where much of the risk might lie. Since certain entities are not regulated, they lack the additional level of scrutiny some may find important when uncertainty enters the markets.

If the markets lose confidence in the sponsors of certain derivatives, traders will try to sell those derivatives even if the underlying asset is doing well. That exacerbates the illiquidity problem. Additionally, certain derivatives which typically move in a correlated manner with each other may no longer correlate as forced sales and issuer risk distort market prices. Thus falling values of leveraged, complex, illiquid securities, combined with a loss in confidence in derivative counterparties, further stimulates a chaotic trading environment.

Many operational issues that financial firms have grappled with during sanguine markets would test them to the limit in a volatile, chaotic market. The need for timely settlements of trades, proper staffing and reliable systems to handle the activity might cause additional problems at some firms. Since major financial institutions play a part in these markets, both through their own proprietary trading desks and through lending activities to hedge funds, a major market dislocation could impact them as well. If markets begin to lose faith in major financial institutions, even the Fed may be unable to restore financial markets.

Chapter 5

Debt and Deficits

When a physician sees a patient who looks and sounds well, a good physician will utilize tools available to him to make sure there are no problems lurking beneath the surface. Likewise, a good economist will look beyond basic measurements of economic health to determine the factors that contributed to the measures and whether or not they are balanced and sustainable.

The most basic measure of economic health is the gross domestic product (GDP), which is the value of the goods and services produced within an economy. GDP is calculated by adding its four major components:

1. Government expenditures
2. Investments
3. Personal consumption expenditures
4. Net exports

In 2005, government spending represented 18% of GDP; investment spending, 17%; and consumer spending, 70%, while net foreign trade had a negative 6% impact on GDP. Economic recoveries, recessions and depressions are defined by the changes in GDP. A recession is usually defined as two consecutive quarters of negative real GDP growth while a depression is considered as a severe form of recession with respect to its length and depth.

In the 24 years since 1982, the US has suffered only 5 quarters of real negative GDP growth, most recently in 2001. Technically, the economic downturn in 2000-2001 did not qualify as a recession since the negative quarters (Q3 2000 -.5%, Q1 2001 -.5% and Q3 2001 -1.4%) were not consecutive. Recessions and downturns are typically deeper than the one experienced in 2001 and more frequent, yet GDP, financial markets and real estate have all performed well over the last several years. To determine the sustainability of this positive trend, one must examine in greater detail the components of GDP from the perspectives of the government, investment, consumer and foreign trade sectors.

Balance sheets and income statements are the core analytical tools used to establish financial standing and capacity for individuals and corporations. Similar tools exist for the government and foreign trade. Generally, whenever an entity's income statement reflects a deficit, an entry is made on its balance sheet, indicating a reduction in net worth. Chronic deficits destroy wealth. As much as governments, corporations or individuals try to camouflage or obfuscate persistent deficits, the charade will only be temporary. Lenders and investors who fund these entities will often times reach a level of discomfort at which point they stop funding them. Sometimes it takes a recession or some other crisis to reveal the rot these deficits cause to the financial standing of an entity or individual. Warren Buffett once said, "It's only when the tide goes out that you learn who's been swimming naked".

US Government Deficits

The budget deficit is the shortfall between the government's revenues (income) and its spending. According to the General Accounting Office (GAO)[42], at the end of fiscal year 2005, the nation's government income statement reflected over $2.9 trillion in spending versus $2.2 trillion in revenue, creating a deficit of $760 billion. Using a different methodology, the government reported a budget deficit of "only" $319 billion after subtracting unfunded liabilities and borrowing money from other government accounts, e.g., Social Security. The more accurate picture of the government's fiscal health is represented by the $760 billion, whereas the $319 billion figure is an indicator of the amount the government must currently raise in the financial markets. The deficit for fiscal 2006 is expected to narrow due to greater tax revenues generated by a stronger economy. The following tables published by the Treasury Department illustrate the source and use of funds for the US government during fiscal years 2004 and 2005.

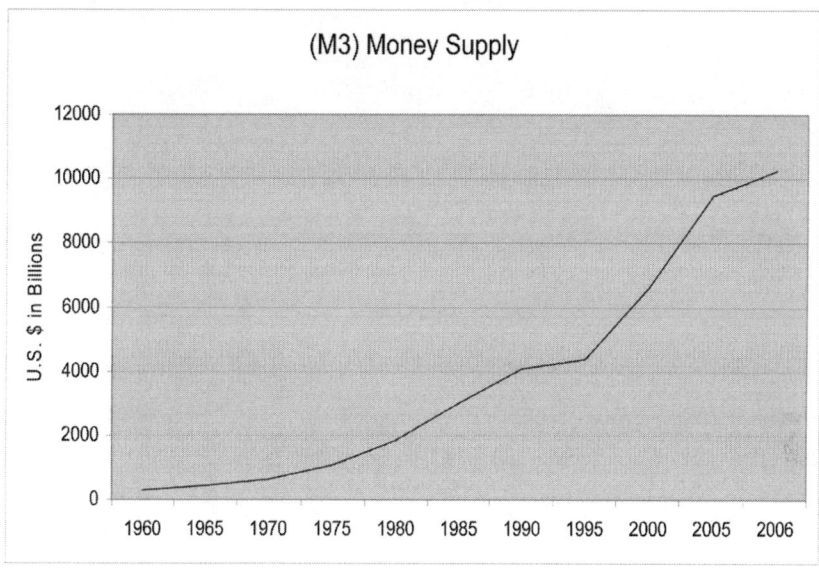

Source: Federal Reserve Data

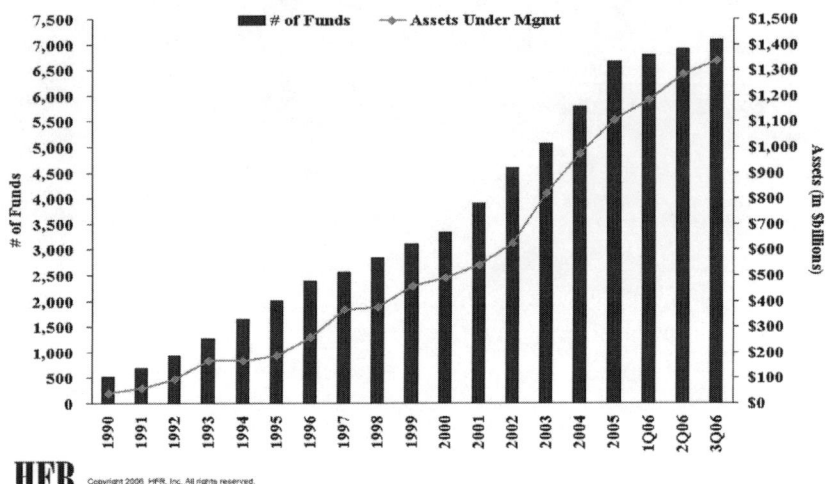

US Government Indebtedness

The national debt is the total of all the money the government owes through the issuance of Treasury bonds, notes and bills to finance the nation's accumulated budget deficits. The GAO reported that at the end of fiscal year 2005, the federal government's balance sheet consisted of total assets of $1.5 trillion and total liabilities of $9.9 trillion for a net position of -$8.4 trillion. However, this figure understates the true extent of government indebtedness. According to Comptroller General David Walker our liabilities as a nation including not only the official debt but also the unfunded promises for Social Security, Medicare and other programs added up to $43 trillion at the end of 2004[43]. This represents a doubling in the nation's liability since 2000, with the new Medicare prescription drug plan alone accounting trillions of dollars in new liabilities. $43 trillion represents $145,000 for every man, woman and child in America!

The modern trend towards deficit financing began in the 1960s when the US waged a war in Vietnam and increased social spending. Federal taxes were cut in the 1980s and government spending increased for the most part from the 1960s through 2006, leading to rising budget deficits and a larger debt burden.

Interest Payment on Existing Debts & Deficits

The US Treasury debt outstanding for 2005 was $7.9 trillion, compared to $2.6 trillion in 1988. Interest payments have become a drain on government resources as deficit spending adds to the national debt, and the cost of financing increases it further.

The following table shows data released by Bureau of the Public Debt regarding interest payments on public debts (US Treasury borrowings) during the past 15 fiscal years ending September 30th, 2006. The chart reflects a growing interest expense burden despite significantly lower interest rates in the past few years.

Historical Data on Interest Expenses and Debts Outstanding

(in $ millions)

Fiscal Year End	Interest expenses	Debt outstanding
2006	$385,017,969,084.24	Not available
2005	$352.350,252,507.90	$7,932,709,661,723.50
2004	$321,566,323,971.29	$7,379,052,696,330.32
2003	$318,148,529,151.51	$6,783,231,062,743.62
2002	$332,536,958,599.42	$6,228,235,965,597.16
2001	$359,507,635,242.41	$5,807,463,412,200.06
2000	$361,997,734,302.36	$5,674,178,209,886.86
1999	$353,511,471,722.87	$5,656,270,901,615.43
1998	$363,823,722,920.26	$5,526,193,008,897.62
1997	$355,795,834,214.66	$5,413,146,011,397.34
1996	$343,955,076,695.15	$5,224,810,939,135.73
1995	$332,413,555,030.62	$4,973,982,900,709.39
1994	$296,277,764,246.26	$4,692,749,910,013.32
1993	$292,502,219,484.25	$4,411,488,883,139.38
1992	$292,361,073,070.74	$4,064,620,655,521.66
1991	$286,021,921,181.04	$3,665,303,351,697.03
1990	$264,852,544,615.90	$3,233,313,451,777.25
1989	$240,863,231,535.71	$2,857,430,960,187.32
1988	$214,145,028,847.73	$2,602,337,712,041.16

Bureau of The Public Debt

Contingent Liabilities

A considerable portion of the contingent liabilities of the federal government are entitlement programs including Social Security, and Medicare & Medicaid. These liabilities are real and substantial, but they are not being adequately funded. The following is a brief description of these sizable programs.

Social Security Payments

Since the introduction of Social Security in 1935 to aid senior citizens, it has grown to become the largest federal program in the country. When the program was originally established, low inflation and life expectancy rates resulted in low cost estimates for the program. Due to increasing inflation in the ensuing decades along with an expansion in longevity, larger amounts were paid to individuals than projected. The issue of Social Security influences many voters' decisions, so successive governments have enlarged the program in terms of coverage and benefits and widened the target groups. The groups now include workers' spouses and minor children, disabled workers and survivors of deceased workers. The amount paid into the program by workers entering the workforce today does not meet the financial requirements needed to ensure the program's existence through their life expectancies.

Medicare

The second largest entitlement program after Social Security, Medicare, provides health insurance coverage to elderly or disabled people. Most Medicare beneficiaries also receive Social Security. Medicare, enacted in 1965, is comprised of two programs – Hospital Insurance (HI) and Supplementary Medical Insurance (SMI). The HI program pays for inpatient care in hospitals, certain other facilities such as skilled nursing facilities, home health care, hospice services, etc. The SMI program pays for services from physicians, medical suppliers and outpatient care facilities, as well as for some home health care.

HI is financed largely by a payroll tax levied on workers and their employers. SMI is financed in two ways: roughly one-quarter of its funding comes from monthly premiums paid by enrollees and the rest from the government's general revenues. In all, beneficiaries pay for less than 15% of current Medicare outlays.

The Congressional Budget Office (CBO) estimates that Medicare's costs as a percentage of GDP will rise from 2.5% in 2003 to 9.2% in 2075. Approximately 30% of that growth is attributed to society's aging and the remaining 70% to the growth of health care costs per enrollee in excess of the rate of growth of GDP per capita

Medicaid

The Medicaid program, also enacted in 1965, is a joint federal/

state program and extends medical assistance to many of the nation's poor people. Payments for long-term care (mainly for the elderly and disabled) account for about one-third of total Medicaid spending. The federal government and the states pay for the program jointly, with the federal government's share ranging from 50% to 83% (depending on a state's per capita income). The source of the funds for this program is largely from the federal government's revenue from payroll taxes. The nature of the funding at present is on a pay-as-you-go basis.

Present Scenario

Social Security benefits alone account for one-fifth of federal spending, and payroll taxes for the program account for one-fourth of federal revenues. Presently, the revenues paid into Social Security are greater than the amounts paid out. Soon, expenditures will exceed revenues. Future liabilities in terms of entitlement funds have received much attention recently and reforms are being considered. If Social Security is going to be reformed, it is important that it be done soon. As time passes, the gap between the present value of future liabilities and the present value of future revenues will only widen further.

At the beginning of this decade, the federal government paid monthly Social Security benefits to more than 45 million retired or disabled workers, their families and their survivors. Those benefits cost the government a total of about $430 billion that year – an amount equivalent to roughly one-quarter of the entire federal budget.

Over the next 30 years, the baby boomers (those born between 1946 and 1964) will retire, increasing the number of potential beneficiaries over the age of 65 by almost 90% – from 36 million in 2000 to 69 million in 2030. This will pose new challenges for the Social Security program, the federal government and the US economy. During the same period, the number of adults under the age of 65 – who will largely be the ones paying the taxes to support their elders – will grow only by about 15% (from 170 million to 195 million). Moreover, the number of elderly people is expected to keep rising at a faster rate than the number of non-elderly people as life spans continue to increase. Another challenge raised by the increase in the elderly is the corresponding increase that would be required of federal health care programs.

A large share of Medicaid payments has gone to provide long-term care for elderly and disabled people in nursing facilities. The federal government's expenditure on Medicare and Medicaid was approximately

$370 billion in 2000. Remember, these programs, together with Social Security, accounted for nearly half of all federal spending, excluding interest payments on federal debt at the beginning of the decade. If the programs are not changed, by 2030, they will consume an estimated two-thirds of the entire federal budget.[44]

Figures released from the Congressional Budget Office show that as a percentage of the GDP, the projected federal spending on Social Security, Medicare and Medicaid is expected to double from 7% in 2000 to 15% in 2030. Social Security Trustees estimate that Social Security will begin to exceed the tax revenues earmarked for the program in 2016. In 2038, it is expected that the Trust Funds will be depleted.

Projected Revenues and Outlays of Social Security and Medicare (As a percentage of GDP): 2002-2075						
	Social Security		Medicare		Social Security and Medicare (Combined)	
Calendar Year	Revenues	Outlays	Revenues	Outlays	Revenues	Outlays
2002	5.2	4.5	1.8	2.5	7.0	6.9
2010	5.1	4.4	1.8	2.5	6.9	7.0
2020	5.1	5.6	2.0	3.3	7.1	8.9
2030	5.1	6.6	2.1	4.5	7.2	11.1
2040	5.0	6.7	2.2	5.4	7.2	12.1
2050	4.9	6.7	2.2	6.0	7.2	12.6
2060	4.8	6.8	2.3	6.8	7.2	13.5
2070	4.8	6.9	2.4	7.9	7.2	14.8
2075	4.7	7.0	2.5	8.4	7.2	15.4

Sources: Social Security Administration, *The 2002 Annual Report of the Board of Trustees of the Federal Old-Age and Survivors Insurance and Disability Insurance Trust Funds* (March 26, 2002); Department of Health and Human Services, Centers for Medicare and Medicaid Services, Office of the Actuary, *2002 Annual Report of the Board of Trustees of the Federal Hospital Insurance and Federal Supplementary Medical Insurance Trust Funds* (March 26, 2002); and supplemental data from both agencies.

A large proportion of the population has come to rely on Social Security to play an integral part in retirement planning and it seems unimaginable for the government to stand by while the trust fund runs out of money. The ultimate solution is bound to involve some form of a reduction in benefits, particularly to those who can afford it, along with an increase in deductions from workers' paychecks, and some budgetary government expenditure. The solution will involve a cost to society since funds will be extracted from the economy in one form or another to keep the program viable. There will also most likely be growing resentment on the part of the future work force as they will be required to carry a heavier burden to supplement retirees' income.

The Medical Modernization Act (MMA 2003)

The MMA 2003 added prescription drug coverage to Medicare beginning January 1, 2006. The elderly and the disabled can enroll in private plans that contract with Medicare to provide a drug benefit. It is estimated that providing prescription coverage to more than 41 million seniors in 2015 will cost more than $107 billion annually[45]. Budget figures released by the White House indicate that the new Medicare prescription drug benefit will cost more than $1.2 trillion in the coming decade, a much higher price tag than President Bush suggested when he narrowly won passage of the law in late 2003.

Pension Benefit Guaranty Corporation (PBGC)

The Pension Benefit Guaranty Corporation (PBGC) was created by the Employee Retirement Income Security Act of 1974 to encourage voluntary and private pension plans by guaranteeing assured payments to pension recipients. PBGC is funded by the insurance premiums it collects from employers that sponsor the pension plans.

The system is flawed in part due to the excessive flexibility given to companies in establishing assumptions when calculating funding levels to match future liabilities, known as funding targets. Companies have flexibility in choosing methodologies to determine current assets and future liabilities. Employers make assumptions such as the discount rate, mortality rate and asset valuation. Also, the plan sponsors have the freedom to not fully fund their liabilities. Since pension liabilities are expense items on financial statements, many companies choose to make certain assumptions and underfund in order to maximize reported profitability, even if they paint an unrealistic picture of the companies' future liabilities. Entities experiencing financial stress are especially likely to underfund their obligations. Such actions have resulted in a troubled PBGC, which may potentially lead to a government bailout.

At the end of fiscal year 2005, the plan had a negative net financial position of -$23 billion, its largest deficit ever, with over 80% of all claims against it occurring from 2000 to 2005. Plan funding levels are at an all-time low while payouts are at an all-time high. The PBGC had to pay retirement checks amounting to over $3.5 billion to 700,000 retirees in fiscal year 2005.

The PBGC insured pension benefits for over 44 million people and faced a potential unfunded liability of $431 billion, although only $108 billion was classified as "reasonably possible" in 2005. Due to the fact it is a government-sponsored institution, its liabilities may ultimately fall on the lap of government. Growing pressure in Washington led to legislation in 2006 that tightened the range of assumptions that can be used by companies. The new law also requires many companies to fund 100% of their pension liabilities in the next few years. Some companies may decide to convert to defined contribution plans rather than face stricter rules and most likely higher premium payments to the PBGC. Although this legislation will slow the bleeding, there is still significant liability in the pipeline that must be covered.

Private Investment

The component of GDP referred to as 'investment' pertains to the purchase of capital goods, or goods used in future production. This definition of investment differs from the one commonly used, which refers to purchases of financial instruments. The value of financial instruments purchased and sold are not included in GDP and are referred to as 'savings' in the economic realm. The investment category of GDP includes plants, equipment, office buildings, inventories, software, computers and residential housing structures. Housing represents approximately 40% of the investment portion of GDP and will be discussed in the next chapter. What remains in the investment category can be evaluated best by analyzing the capacity, desire and action on the part of the corporate sector.

To gauge the financial capacity of corporations to embark on capital spending projects, various ratios can be examined involving assets, cash, debt, etc. Clearly, some companies are healthier than others, but when taken in aggregate, the conclusion is that corporate America is healthier now than it has been for some time. The investment boom in the late 1990s led to an increase in productivity and profitability. A prolonged period of low interest rates and low spreads between treasury and corporate yields, along with high stock prices, resulted in corporations taking action to strengthen their balance sheets by refinancing or paying off debts. At the end of 2004, non-financial corporations had $21.1 trillion in assets and $10.1 in liabilities for an aggregate net worth of $11 trillion. The aggregate liquidity and debt to equity ratios and interest expense coverages are the strongest they have been in many years. Corporate balance sheets have the capacity for expansion of capital spending, however we must next ascertain their desire to act and then how their actions or lack thereof will impact the economy.

Towards the end of 2006, a growing number of economists expressed their concern that consumer spending was unlikely to continue growing. If consumer-oriented industries begin to lose confidence in demand for their goods, it is unlikely they will spend money on increasing capacity. Many industries are still feeling the after-effects of the capital spending boom experienced in the 1990s. For most of the 1990s equipment spending increased by double digits, resulting in unprecedented post-WWII growth. Additionally, the rapid rise in industrial capacity in lower cost regions around the world must also be considered for companies operating in a globally competitive environment. In fact, many US companies have embraced lower operating costs overseas by establishing foreign production facilities. Even though this may increase the profitability for companies, dollars earmarked for capacity expansion spent overseas rather than domestically will lead to a shrinkage in the fixed investment component of GDP.

Although capital spending has increased from 2002 to 2006, it is below trend, given the strength in this recovery. Many companies have opted to acquire other companies or purchase shares of their own stock. Approximately $742 billion was spent by corporate America in the two year period from Q4 of 2004 through Q3 of 2006 on stock repurchases[46]. The countervailing forces discussed should keep the impact of non-residential investment on GDP somewhat muted, especially since it only represents about 10% of GDP without housing.

Consumer Spending

Consumer spending is the largest contributing sector to GDP by an overwhelming margin and has grown more rapidly in the last few years than the overall economy. Representing a record 70% of GDP, the consumer sector must be examined carefully to access its sustainability. The evidence indicates that the growth in consumer spending over the past several years has been fueled largely by debt, not income, casting its sustainability in doubt.

Growth in personal income from 2000 to Q2 2006 was 32% while growth in consumption expenditures was 40%. The difference came out of savings and inflated assets, causing the national savings rate to dip below zero in 2005 for the first time since the Great Depression. The savings rate remained negative during the first half of 2006. The recent descent is a continuation of a downward trend in national savings from 9% in the 1980s to 5% in the 1990s to our present negative rate. Debt used for consumption is spending today what you must pay back with future earnings. So although spending levels observed in isolation may lead one to assume the economy is healthy, the fact that the source of funds for spending is largely from debt leads to less future economic activity.

Abundant and inexpensive capital made available to consumers by the financial system, in part due to inflating asset prices, has provided the means to spend. Total net new borrowings by the household sector grew from $300 billion in 1997 to $1.24 trillion in 2005 according to the Federal Reserve's Flow of Funds Report. Consumers' net worth, however, has grown as asset growth has kept pace. Looking at the numbers in aggregate, the Federal Reserve reported total household net worth at $53.5 trillion or $178,000 per capita in the second quarter of 2006. The net worth figure is the difference between total household assets of $66 trillion and total household liabilities of $12.7 trillion. Almost one-third of household assets consist of real estate holdings and most of the rest consists of financial assets including cash and securities. The bulk of the liability side resides in mortgage debt, although credit card and other forms of consumer debt have grown rapidly to significant levels. A primary reason asset levels have kept pace with rising debt is the dramatic increase in home values over the past several years. If we are in a housing bubble, however, those gains could be illusory, while the debt is very real and will not simply disappear.

The sustainability of consumers' growth in consumption is predicated on either an increase in real wages or a continued increase in asset levels, along with monetization of those increases. It is difficult to imagine a substantial increase in real wages when a globally competitive environment offers labor arbitrage opportunities to many employers. With respect to asset prices, namely housing, a continued upward trend is unlikely and will be discussed in detail in the next chapter.

The Trade Balance

In 2005, the US exported $1.3 trillion and imported $2.0 trillion in goods and services, resulting in a trade deficit of over $700 billion. Trade deficits subtract from GDP, so even though the excess is consumed here, it is produced in another country. The $700 billion deficit resulted in a 6% reduction in GDP.

As global trade has increased over the years, US exports have also increased, although imports have increased at a faster rate, resulting in widening deficits. Since the money used to pay for net imports flows in the opposite direction of goods and services, a transfer of wealth typically occurs between countries as deficits persist. If a significant portion of imports is for capital goods, the result may be an enhancement of future productivity, leading to increased exports and a more balanced trade condition. However, if a country's imports are for non-productive consumption, imbalances will likely become more conspicuous. Capital goods imports in the US have declined as a percentage of imports in the past few years.

A persistent trade deficit results in an accumulation of claims against the importing country. At the end of 2005, foreign investors held a net $5.8 trillion worth of US financial assets more than US investors held in foreign financial assets. The US became a net debtor to foreign investors in 1985 for the first time since WWII and that debt has grown larger ever since. Foreign investors, including central banks, held 47% of all outstanding US Treasuries, 15% of US agencies, 29% of US corporate bonds, and 7% of all US stocks at the end of 2005 (See the followig table)[47]. A little over a decade earlier, foreigners owned less than half of those percentages. The trend is continuing as 97% of the $307 billion in net new Treasury bond issuance in 2005 and 99% of the $363 billion issued in 2004 was snapped up by foreigners[48]. In other words, the net amount of Treasuries (old and new) purchased by foreigners represented nearly the entire net new issuance of Treasuries in those periods.

In a February 2005 speech, Alan Greenspan referred to the unanticipated decline in long-term rates while the Fed was raising short-term rates as "a conundrum"[49]. That foreign entities have purchased the equivalent of virtually all Treasury bond issuance in 2004 and 2005 identifies the mechanism of the solution to Greenspan's puzzle, but the foreign investor's motive and rationale must be determined in order to fully solve it.

Major Foreign Holders of Treasury Securities

	Country	Amount Held (in Billions of $)	
		12.31.05	9.30.06
1.	Japan	669.0	639.2
2.	Mainland China	310.0	342.1
3.	United Kingdom	146.0	207.8
4.	Caribbean Banking Centers	78.6	52.7
5.	Taiwan	68.1	65.0
6.	Germany	49.9	52.4
7.	OPEC	78.2	103.4
8.	Korea	69.0	69.0
9.	Canada	27.8	49.7
10.	Hong Kong	40.3	49.7

Source: Department of the Treasury / Federal Reserve Board

Estimated foreign holdings of U.S. Treasury marketable and non-marketable bills, bonds, and notes reported under the Treasury International Capital (TIC) reporting system are based on annual Surveys of Foreign Holdings of U.S. Securities and on monthly data.

Some authorities, including Fed Chairman Bernanke, have claimed that the US Current Account deficit (trade deficit net of interest, dividends and cash grants) is a result of a global savings glut[50]. Excess savings from around the world enter the US, widening the current account deficit. US markets are deep and liquid, and we have a stable government and strong military. These factors serve to make the dollar the world reserve currency, attracting capital to the US. However, the savings glut argument is circular in that much of the global savings glut was generated by US consumption of foreign produced goods. US per capita consumption is significantly higher and saving significantly lower than other countries and is largely a cultural issue. Excess consumption must carry a large share of the blame for our current account deficits.

There is a desire on the part of several foreign governments to manipulate the dollar's value in relation to their currencies, to maintain export competitiveness. This operation involves the recycling of dollars received from their exports back into US securities. If instead, they sold their dollars in the currency markets in exchange for their own currencies, the price of the dollar would decline and export prices would rise as more depreciated dollars would be required to purchase the same items. This would potentially lead to a decrease in exports into the US, a situation many export-dependent countries do not want to see.

The preceding reasons should answer the question as to how foreigners rationalize their decisions to continue buying US securities, thus solving Greenspan's conundrum. But will foreigners continue to finance our increasing debt? That is a key question that requires a closer examination of the issues facing foreign investors.

Foreign institutions and individuals must consider currency risk in addition to the same risks our domestic investors consider, i.e., rising interest rates, inflation, economic conditions, etc. For example, assume a Japanese investor spends $1 million for a one year Treasury note yielding 4% interest, the return in dollars to the investor is $1,040,000 when the note matures. If we further assume the yen appreciates 10% against the dollar over the same period, the investor will lose money after translating it back to his own currency. So 10% of the $1,040,000 or $104,000 is lost in the currency exchange, resulting in a return of $936,000 yen equivalent to the investor, a net loss of $64,000.

Central banks working in concert with their governments must consider the potential problem of having an excess concentration in dollar-denominated paper, especially when the dollar is vulnerable. These uncertainties are weighed against a desire for export competitiveness. An artificially high dollar also benefits US consumers with artificially low prices for imported goods and it benefits US capital markets with artificially low interest rates. Today's state of "co-dependency" on an artificially strong dollar has been referred to as a kind of Bretton Woods II system of currency management. The real Bretton Woods agreement (refer to Chapter 2) was signed in 1944 and tied global currencies to the US dollar, which was anchored through its convertibility into gold. So far investors, foreign producers and domestic US consumers have been the beneficiaries of this Bretton Woods II system at the expense of domestic producers and foreign consumers. Ultimately, managing the value of the major global currency at artificial levels will misshape the financial signals private industry and consumers rely upon in making economic decisions, particularly when the reference currency is untethered to anything such as gold.

If some analysts are correct in assessing the Chinese yuan as 20-30% undervalued against the US dollar, then the Chinese enjoy an approximate price advantage of that percentage simply from the distortion in currency translation. To examine how China fixes its currency's value against the dollar despite massive exports, we will follow the money using an example. Assume you walk into your local Wal-Mart and purchase $100 worth of trinkets made in China. You hand a $100 bill to the cashier, which is later deposited into Wal-Mart's bank account. Wal-Mart then reorders the trinkets you removed from the shelf from its Chinese supplier. The supplier does not want dollars since he must pay for his raw materials, labor and other expenses in yuan, so he exchanges the dollars for yuan at his local Chinese bank. The bank has no need for dollars either, so it exchanges its dollars for yuan at the Chinese central bank.

The buck stops here. The central bank does not dare sell the dollars in the open market or else the dollar will decline against the yuan, making China's goods more expensive. Japan and other countries also conduct these operations, but even central banks can grow weary of sustaining losses associated with a declining dollar. The action of maintaining their currencies at unsustainably low levels has caused problems in their own economies, like inflation and over-investment in capacity, leading to bad loans and problems in their banking systems.

Nouriel Roubini, professor of Economics and International Business at the Stern School of Business, sees an unstable environment posed by the large US current account deficit and the management of the dollar[51]. He points to the scale of financial flows required to sustain the new 'Bretton Woods II' as the Achilles heel which can destabilize the existing precarious system. According to Roubini this new regime will not prove to be stable. He claimed that interest rates foreigners were receiving on US securities (at least those that prevailed in 2004) were too low relative to the risk of future dollar declines. The amount of reserve accumulation needed is too much of a burden for the small group of central banks to be sustained for long. At current deficit rates of $700-$800 billion per year needing to be financed, the incentive for some central banks to cheat will increase over time. Aside from direct potential losses if the dollar declines, some governments are also leery of their own overheated economies and the long-term problems that can create.

As the economy demands larger doses of liquidity, more debt must be created to maintain growth. It is unlikely foreigners will continue to build ever larger positions of US debt. Even if we could continue to depend on the 'kindness of strangers' to support our spending addiction, the result would be to transfer increasing amounts of our wealth to other countries. Once again, I wish to rely on Warren Buffett's unique storytelling ability to reduce complex economic ideas into an easy to comprehend format. The following is another excerpt from Warren Buffett's report to shareholders of Berkshire Hathaway, dated February 28, 2005:

> "...the exchange of goods and services with other countries – is enormously beneficial for both us and them. Last year we had $1.15 trillion of such honest-to-God trade and the more of this, the better. But, as noted, our country also purchased an additional $618 billion in goods and services from the rest of the world that was unreciprocated. That is a staggering figure and one that has important consequences. The balancing item to this one-way pseudo-trade – in economics there is always an offset – is a transfer of wealth from the U.S. to the rest of the world. The transfer may materialize in the form of IOUs our private or governmental institutions give to foreigners, or by way of their assuming ownership of our assets, such as stocks and real estate. In either case, Americans end up owning a reduced portion of our country while non-Americans own a greater part. This force-feeding of American wealth to the rest of the world is now proceeding at the rate of $1.8 billion daily, an increase of 20% since I wrote you last year. Consequently, other countries and their citizens now own a net of about $3 trillion of the U.S. A decade ago their net ownership was negligible..."
>
> "...As a rich 'family' awash in goods, Americans will argue through their legislators as to how government should redistribute the national output – that is who pays taxes and who receives governmental benefits. If 'entitlement' promises from an earlier day have to be reexamined, 'family members' will angrily debate among themselves as to who feels the pain. Maybe taxes will go up; maybe promises will be 'modified' maybe more internal debt will be issued. But when the fight is finished, all of the family's huge pie remains available for its members, however it is divided. No slice must be sent abroad.
>
> Large and persisting current account deficits produce an entirely different result. As time passes, and as claims against us grow, we own less and less of what we produce. In effect, the rest of the world enjoys an ever-growing royalty on American output. Here, we are like a family that consistently overspends its income. As time passes, the family finds that it is working more and more for the 'finance company' and less for itself.
>
> Should we continue to run current account deficits comparable to those now prevailing, the net ownership of the U.S. by other countries and

their citizens a decade from now will amount to roughly $11 trillion. And, if foreign investors were to earn only 5% on that net holding, we would need to send a net of $0.55 trillion of goods and services abroad every year merely to service the U.S. investments then held by foreigners. At that date, a decade out, our GDP would probably total about $18 trillion (assuming low inflation, which is far from a sure thing). Therefore, our U.S. 'family' would then be delivering 3% of its annual output to the rest of the world simply as tribute for the overindulgences of the past. In this case, unlike that involving budget deficits, the sons would truly pay for the sins of their fathers.

This annual royalty paid to the world – which would not disappear unless the U.S. massively underconsumed and began to run consistent and large trade surpluses – would undoubtedly produce significant political unrest in the U.S. Americans would still be living very well, indeed better than now because of the growth in our economy. But they would chafe at the idea of perpetually paying tribute to their creditors and owners abroad. A country that is now aspiring to an 'Ownership Society' will not find happiness in – and I'll use hyperbole here for emphasis – a 'Sharecropper's Society.' But that's precisely where our trade policies, supported by Republicans and Democrats alike, are taking us.

Many prominent U.S. financial figures, both in and out of government, have stated that our current-account deficits cannot persist. For instance, the minutes of the Federal Reserve Open Market Committee of June 29-30, 2004 say: 'The staff noted that outsized external deficits could not be sustained indefinitely.' But despite the constant handwringing by luminaries, they offer no substantive suggestions to tame the burgeoning imbalance."[32]

Chapter 6

The Dynamics of a Bubble

The word 'bubble' is employed to describe a large and rapid increase in asset prices (stocks, bonds, real estate, commodities, etc.) that is not justified by economic fundamentals. The word is used because prices extend to such a level that they eventually pop and collapse. A bubble exists when investors buy assets at prices above their fundamental values, with the expectation of selling them at even higher prices in the future.

Investment asset prices, by their nature, vary over time. Although analysts can venture an educated guess as to what an asset's price range should be, whether or not it trades in that range is almost as much art as science. Since the relationship between asset prices and values lacks precision, we cannot classify everything that veers above our expected price levels as bubbles. However, when one considers the fundamentals of the asset along with financial conditions, trends, historical correlations and future outlook, it is possible to establish a reasonable price expectation. At times, certain asset prices move so far above logical price levels that analysts not caught up in the hysteria and exercising common sense can recognize it as a bubble.

A bubble can more easily develop today because we have a monetary system that is not restrained by a gold standard, an accommodating Federal Reserve and a financial services industry which helps provide the necessary liquidity by buying large amounts of debt obligations.

The preconditions that lead to the formation and reinforcement of bubbles are:

1. Abundant liquidity
2. A compelling theme and
3. Persistent price momentum.

In order to fuel the rise in an asset class, continuous and increasingly excessive liquidity directed to that asset class is necessary. This is most likely to occur with a backdrop of loose monetary policy from the Federal Reserve. New and large liquidity flows are often characterized by new lenders entering that market, liberalized lending policies relating to the class and active speculator fund flows (hedge funds and others). However, one must realize that liquidity conditions will change over time.

Another precondition for bubble formation is a compelling theme or story that justifies why the asset will demonstrate a continuously increasing price. The story usually contains an element of rarity or limited supply, such as: "they aren't making any more land". The story may also argue for the asset's continuous demand ".... will change our lives forever" where one can fill in the blank with technologies such as TV, radio, plastics, or the internet, among others. Often, the theme involves changing innovations, like railroads in the 19th century. Or the story may relate to something unique, such as the Dutch tulips which created a mania in the 17th century. Although some of these themes may be credible, they do not guarantee profits. The dimension of price must always be considered.

Once liquidity meets a good story, prices begin to move. Early investors tend to do well, temporarily reinforcing expectations. If an increase in prices is expected, sellers hold back their supply and prices tend to gather momentum. A certain bravado takes hold as early investors willingly share their experience with others at cocktail parties, attracting new investors in the process, and a 'buzz' is created. At some point, the trend begins to show up on the media's radar and then prices begin to enter the manic phase. New entrepreneurs enter the field while others leave their jobs to stake their claims in the newly vibrant industry as salespeople, secretaries or other support staff. At this point, everyone pities the poor lonely soul at the cocktail party who hasn't at least passively invested in the frenzy. At this point, speculators would be foolish to stay in the game. Market forces dictate that when public sentiment is overwhelmingly aligned, price trends are about to change.

When contemplating the initiation or continuance of an investment in an asset undergoing bubble dynamics, keep in mind that:

1. Liquidity conditions change
2. Themes change
3. Trends change

4. A consideration of price levels must be made in relation to fundamental values.

Liquidity conditions can change both on a macro level with the Federal Reserve's intervention, or on a narrower level with respect to flows within the inflating asset class. When a bubble grows large enough, it can impact the overall economy. Excessive speculation will lead to artificially high prices for the asset class and can lead to broader inflation within the economy. A responsive and alert central bank would act prior to a bubble reaching this stage to head off the more serious consequences of acting too late. However, if a bubble is allowed to get too far, the Federal Reserve would have little choice than to head off broader inflation by moving quickly to burst it with tighter monetary conditions and higher interest rates.

If general inflation has already set in, the Federal Reserve would have to extricate inflationary sentiment by a more protracted period of interest rates rising at a more aggressive pace. Other consequences of acting too slowly or not aggressively enough are accumulations of questionable investments and speculative flows that occur during the bubble expansion. Once real monetary tightening begins, these misallocated flows become problematic. High real (net of inflation) interest rates are the silver bullets that can blow up overleveraged speculative positions.

Even if the macro liquidity condition is positive, flows can still stop moving into the bubble, causing it to burst. For example, there could be a disruption in the financial infrastructure used to fund the bubble by an active financial company sustaining large losses through mismanagement or malfeasance. Or a problem could develop with certain leveraged instruments used in this type of finance. Or there could be an emergence of a competing asset class for speculative flows. The more complex the financial framework causing the bubble, the greater the variety of potential mishaps.

An investment theme will only carry an asset class so far. Although quips like "they aren't making any more land" may be true, it is often difficult to profit from the trend. One must consider that prices may already reflect future expectations. The amount paid represents 50% of the profit equation, yet many people choose to ignore it, focusing only on the amount they expect to achieve upon sale of the asset. Trends do not continue to rise in a straight line. In fact, they seem to have a proclivity to temporarily reverse course at just the time that enthusiasm reaches temporary heights, resulting in losses for latecomers. Thus, the timing of short-term trading can be difficult. Other factors impacting trends are competitive forces within the asset type or substitution, competing bubbles, obsolescence and changing consumer tastes or spending patterns.

Regardless of how good a story sounds or how strong a trend may appear, one must always perform a basic fundamental analysis of the asset to determine a reasonable expected price range. Buying a rising, overvalued asset, then expecting to be able to sell the asset to someone else who shares the same disregard of fundamentals at a higher price, is known as the greater fool theory, and it just doesn't work.

Bubbles often give the illusion of a healthy economy. Ample financial liquidity promotes a prosperous economic backdrop, eventually leading increasingly optimistic investors to assume ever-increasing financial risk and speculation. Since bubbles are self-reinforcing, the ensuing speculation becomes unsustainable in the long run and subsequently bursts, often bringing devastating consequences for the broader economy.

History of Bubbles

History is replete with several examples of such bubbles. Some of the prominent ones include the Dutch Tulip mania (1634-1637), when the price of tulip bulbs rose dramatically. At the peak of the mania, the value of special tulip bulbs exceeded the value of a house. But ultimately, prices collapsed, bringing financial ruin to many people throughout the Netherlands. The Mississippi Bubble in Paris and the South Sea Bubble in London (1719-1720) told a similar tale of euphoria-turned-to-panic and devastation. Another big bubble that burst was the Japanese real estate and stock markets in 1989. At home, we had the Railroad Mania (1846-1847), and the stock market bubble of the roaring 1920s, which lead to Great Depression. Recently, we have seen the 1980s' Real Estate Bubbles in Florida and California and the 1990s' bubble in high-tech and telecom stocks. An analysis of a couple of these bubbles will help us to understand the nature and impact that they can have on the economy.

Tulip mania bubble

In 1593, a Viennese botany professor Conrad Guestner brought tulip bulbs to Holland from Turkey. Over the next decade, the tulip became a popular but expensive item in Dutch gardens. In the 17th century, these flowers were stricken with a non-fatal virus known as the mosaic, which had the interesting effect of causing the tulip petals to develop attractively colored stripes. People became infatuated with these beautiful flowers, which led to an increasingly high demand for them. The more unique the tulip, the greater was its value. With 'tulip mania' gripping the country, tulip bulb prices spiraled out of control. The more expensive the bulbs became, the more people viewed them as 'must-have' investments and irrationally extrapolated price trends into the future.

Other sectors of the economy were neglected in favor of speculation in tulip bulbs as people believed that the demand for tulips would continue and that people from around the world would soon join in the craze. As people watched their friends make enormous profits, the temptation to participate in the trend was irresistible. In the last years of the tulip craze, people bartered their personal belongings, land, jewels and furniture to make investments they thought would make them rich. At the height of the frenzy, some tulips were said to have sold for the equivalent of $76,000 in today's dollars.

As with all speculative crazes, prices eventually collapsed. Many investors went bankrupt and most bulbs became worthless, selling for no more than the price of an onion. Aside from telling us that greed transcends time and location, this story illustrates that greed can blind us just as readily as fear can. In this case, it robbed a large part of an entire nation's wealth. Beyond the personal tragedies it caused, the bubble inflicted great damage on the entire Dutch economy.

Japanese bubble

In the aftermath of the devastating impact of WWII on Japan's economy, a new economic model was adopted with the blessings of the Allied powers. Central to the plan was government intervention and economic protection of its domestic industries. As Japan's economy grew into one of the world's strongest over the ensuing decades, these programs began to cause problems with its trading partners, and even in its own economy through the formation of bubbles, which we will discuss shortly. During the 1970s, Japanese stocks and real estate began attracting global attention as prices began a persistent rise. Japan became a leader of technological advancements in the fields of manufacturing, consumer electronics and automobiles. The Japanese were early adopters of new technologies and innovations and they 'borrowed' ideas from other manufacturing countries.

At the same time, Japan began adopting certain scientific management principles. The role of the corporations within the economy was redefined by the government to align their goals with the national interest. In exchange, the government provided financial assistance and reduced taxes, and implemented protectionist policies from foreign competition to encourage corporate investment. Corporations took up joint research projects at the urging of government, to avoid redundancies and overlapping scientific research. Linkages were established along production lines with raw material suppliers, producers and distribution agencies working in a coordinated manner. This systematic planning of economic functions resulted in the ability of Japanese companies to earn high profit margins in the protected domestic market, allowing for lower margins in the highly competitive international markets. The economy was managed by government and industry to become a global exporting powerhouse.

As the economy became reliant on its vibrant export industry, officials became alarmed when after the Plaza Accord of 1985, the yen's value trended higher and negatively impacted its export competitiveness. The Japanese central bank promptly began to ease monetary policy to lower the yen. Money supply increased on average over 10% per year from 1986 to 1990. Between 1986 and 1987, the bank cut rates in half from 5% to 2.5%. This dramatic reduction in short-term interest rates stimulated increases in prices of stocks, bonds and real estate. Speculation set in and asset prices blossomed into a full-blown bubble. Even the stock market crash in the US and other countries in late 1987 did not stop the momentum. At the peak of the Japanese bubble, the Imperial Palace and the land it stood on was said to be worth more than all the land in California, and the market value of all the real estate in Tokyo was worth as much as the market value of real estate in the entire US. The Nikkei 225 index peaked at over 70 times earnings or almost 5 times the average PE ratio in the US market over the previous 100-year period. No rational justification could be made to validate this condition.

Beginning in 1989, the Japanese central bank finally took action to rein in the rampant asset inflation and embarked on a series of five increases in interest rates to 6%. Following the rate increases, the markets collapsed. The stock market fell over 60% from 40,000 in 1989 to under 15,000 in 1990. In 2006, some 16 years later – the Nikkei remained near 15,000. The real estate market fell over 75% from 1991 to 1998. Almost a decade later, Japanese real estate is still struggling to regain its footing.

If, instead of raising rates in 1989, the Japanese central bank had allowed the bubbles to further expand by continuing an accommodative monetary policy, asset prices might have stayed higher for a time, further distorting an obviously untenable balance. Ultimately, even without central bank intervention, the markets would have corrected, but with much greater severity, probably by destroying the value of the country's currency. A central bank can manage to keep interest rates down or it can manage to keep the value of its currency up, but it cannot do both at the same time.

Some of the issues that placed Japan in its predicament are present in our economy today. Like Japan in the 1980s and even the US in the roaring 1920s, the booms were in large part artificially created through credit expansion and speculation. Interest rates were pushed lower and money supply increased by the respective central banks. These actions set the stage for the formation of bubbles which ultimately collapsed.

Real Estate Bubble?

Some economists suggest that due to its enormous size and rapid growth, the US housing market is in a price bubble that surpasses other financial bubbles experienced in world history. At the same time, other economists claim that housing is not in a bubble at all. They say that although certain regions may experience excessive price moves due to various reasons, nationally the housing industry is functioning normally. They attribute the rapid run-up in prices to a shortage of land in desirable locations, environmental restrictions on construction activity, a growing economy and low interest rates. They claim it would be difficult to ever experience a real estate bubble since the cost of transactions is high — approximately 10% if one includes real estate commissions, loan fees, moving expenses, etc. versus only 1-2% for stock transactions. And although housing turnover has recently risen to 6%, the turnover activity on the NYSE is about 100% per year. In addition, the stock market allows for shorting stocks and investing in derivatives, which can accelerate a downward move in prices, whereas the real estate market lacks any such equivalent.

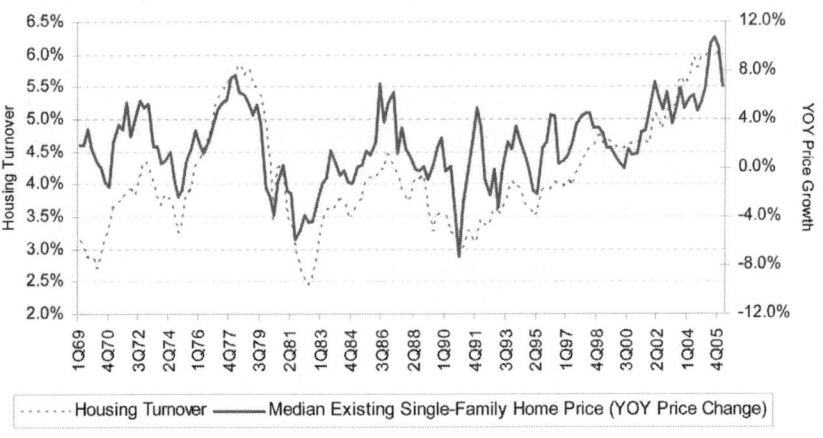

Source: Bureau of Labor and Statistics, National Association of Realtors, and U.S. Census Bureau and Citigroup Investment Research – U.S. Equity Strategy

Are these factors sufficient to disregard talk of a real estate bubble or has the US economy morphed from a stock market bubble into a housing bubble over the last few years? I will argue for the latter. To properly analyze these questions, one must consider housing price changes, their effect on affordability and changes in various valuation measures. We must also examine activity in the financial sector with regard to housing. Finally, an analysis of the implications a possible housing bubble could have on the overall economy is an especially important consideration.

Increase in Housing Prices

The current median price for a home (one-half sold for more and one-half sold for less) in the US has grown from $20,000 in 1968 to $185,000 in 2004. But by the end of 2005, this grew by an additional 14% year over year to $213,000. (The median size of a house also increased from 1,535 square feet in 1975 to 2,140 square feet in 2004, according to figures released by the Census Bureau.) A report by the Center for Economic and Policy Research (CEPR)[53] says that housing prices increased as much as other goods and services from 1950-1995, but since 1995, housing prices have risen by more than 45% **after** adjusting for CPI inflation. Such a massive increase in housing prices over the inflation rate has no precedent.

In 2005, an OFHEO report[54] stated that the increase in the average nominal US home price in the 12 months ending August of 2005 was the **largest one-year increase in more than 25 years**. The report attributed the increase to continued low interest rates and the impact of speculative investment in housing. The housing price index (HPI), which gauges housing price appreciation trends by measuring the housing price changes in repeat sales or refinancing of the same single family home, has also witnessed the largest increase in over 25 years.

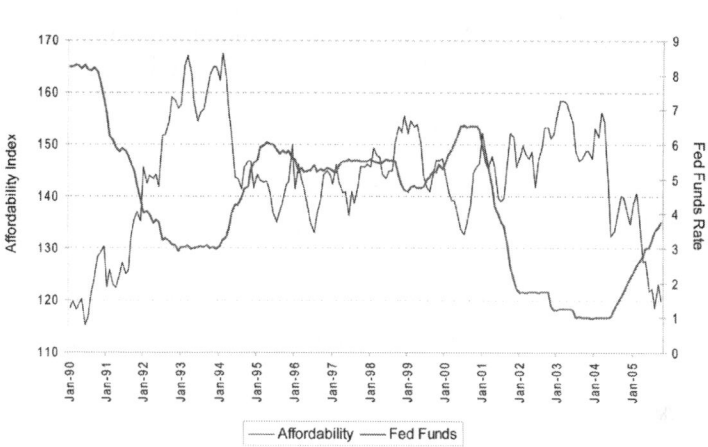

Another measure is the price-to-rent ratio, which is the amount a house could earn if it was rented divided by the value of the house[55]. It is similar to a stock's PE ratio, which is the most popular stock valuation measure. The average PE ratio for housing as an investment stood at a lofty 27 in 2005. *(See the following graph)* When one overlays the "housing PE" from 2000 to 2005 to the NASDAQ PE from 1995 to 2000, a similar pattern emerges. We hope that the similarity ends there because after reaching its peak in 2000 the NASDAQ composite index plunged 80% to its trough in 2002 back down to near its 1995 level. Although the magnitude of the PE expansion was significantly greater for the NASDAQ, a reversion to 2000 levels for the housing PE would have a large impact on many homeowners.

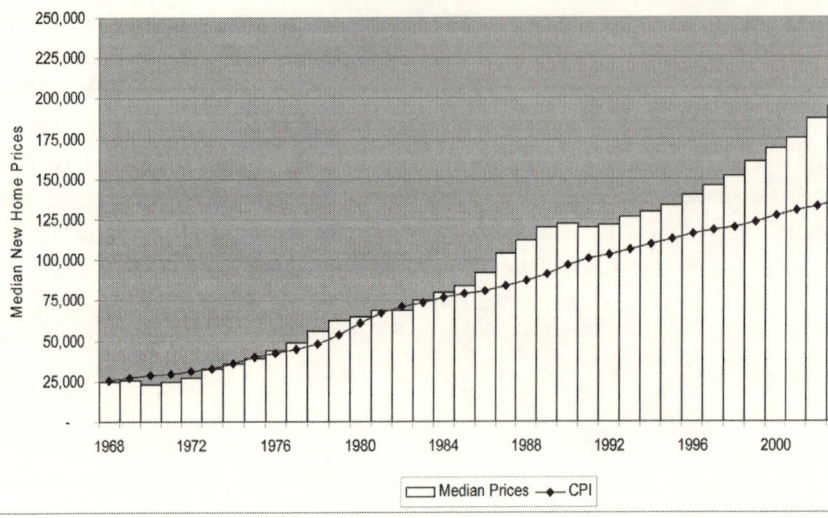

Median New Home Prices vs. CPI (indexed to 1968)

Housing affordability

Housing has become less affordable in recent years. According to a Dallas Fed report[56], in recent years the median income in the US was 130% of the income needed to qualify to buy a median priced home, but by 2005, that figure fell to 120% despite persistently low mortgage rates. In other words, the actual US median income was only 120% of the minimum needed to qualify for a median priced home. If interest rates rise just 1% from 2005 levels this figure would drop to about 110% — well below the range recorded over the past several years. These numbers, however, understate the problem in that they assume one mortgage and conventional rates. But in fact, 13% of home sales in 2005 were for second homes, meaning additional mortgages were taken out by many individuals.

Home buyers and homeowners alike have flocked in recent years to Adjustable Rate Mortgages (ARMs). An FDIC report[57] released in May 2005 said that ARMs accounted for roughly 46% of the value of new mortgages in 2004. The report also warns: "These trends suggest that highly-leveraged borrowers are increasingly taking on interest-rate risk as they stretch to afford high-cost housing."

ARM payments typically adjust annually according to market interest rates after an initial three- or five-year period. Oftentimes, special teaser rates are offered for the initial period before the first reset occurs. Since many people took out ARMs in the last few years when interest rates were low, payments are expected to increase, potentially making them unaffordable for many marginal borrowers. The Mortgage Bankers Association estimates that approximately $330 billion worth of adjustable mortgages in 2006 and $1 trillion worth in 2007 will reset[58]. Others estimate an additional $1 trillion will reset in 2008. Unless interest rates decline from 2006 levels, many people with traditional ARMs will see increasing monthly payments of 25% or more.

To illustrate the impact on monthly payments a rise in rates can have, consider purchasing or refinancing a home using a variable rate mortgage in 2002. If an individual took out a 4.5% variable rate on a $200,000 30-year mortgage, his payments would be $1013 per month. Using the prevailing rates in 2006, he would be paying a new 6.5% rate, translating to payments of $1264 per month. Payments on interest-only loans, used by many sub-prime borrowers, will increase even more. Rising interest rates, coupled with a decline in housing prices, could trigger a spate of distress sales to raise money to pay off housing loans or to minimize risks. This, in turn, could drive prices even lower, with supply outstripping demand. If housing prices fall, bankruptcies will increase. Homeowners leading extravagant lifestyles based on 'equity extraction' *(discussed later)* or those overreaching to buy a home above their means may find themselves in trouble.

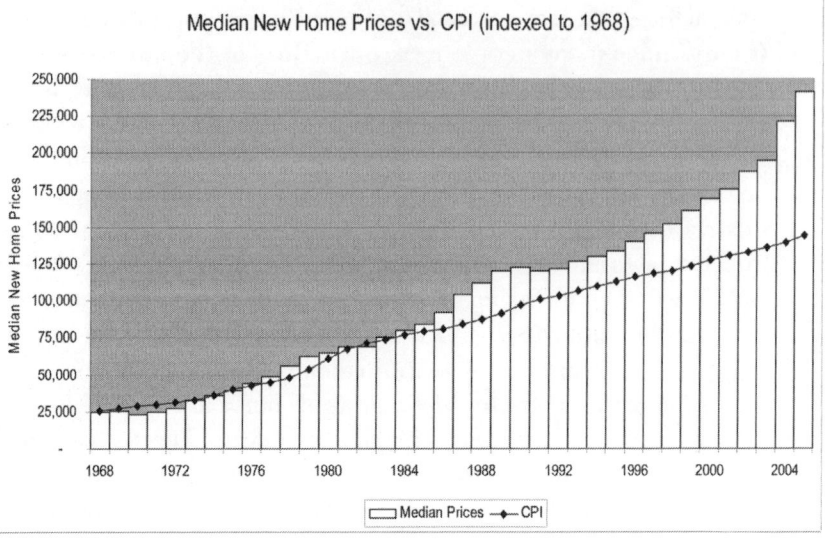

Source: Bureau of Labor Statistics, National Association of Realtors, and U.S. Census Bureau

Housing Supply

The boom in housing construction and sales is evidenced by a CEPR report which states that while the total value of family-owned homes was $18.5 trillion in 2005, over $6.5 trillion of that was generated only in the preceding 8 years through appreciation and new homes constructed.[59]

Home ownership levels are at a record high. The department of Housing and Urban Development (HUD) reported that out of the 107,775,000 occupied housing units in the US, a record 70% are self-owned[60]. The pace of housing construction over the three years 2003-2005 was 40%, higher than the average construction rate in the 17 prior years. Yet, baby boomers are reaching an age where the percentage of income devoted to housing typically declines sharply.

Supply of funds available for housing

So far, there has been little trouble in making funds available for housing. Total housing mortgage debt levels in 2005 were over $8 trillion, up from $7.4 trillion in 2004. But that situation may change. When the yield curve between the 3-month treasuries and the 10-year bond flattens as it did in 2005 and 2006, the supply of funds available for mortgages tends to decline since profit margins for lenders are reduced. This is because banks and other financial companies tend to borrow short-term funds and lend longer term to the mortgage market, earning the difference between the rates. When faced with narrow spreads, the margin for error is reduced, so the focus on the part of lenders traditionally shifts instead to reducing risk. If a flat yield curve persists, available financing may wane.

Signs of Froth in Housing

In an interview with SmartMoney in 2004[61], fabled investor Sir John Templeton said that 20% of people with mortgages are likely to lose their home in foreclosure. Sir John, a 1934 Yale graduate and Rhodes Scholar, is considered by many as one of the wisest investors of all time. He believes that an increase in the number of foreclosed homes sold at auctions would drive down the prices of other homes saying that "a 50% decline in US home prices in quite possible."

The Re-fi Boom

Low interest rates have driven increased housing construction and household consumption. The process of 'equity extraction' has allowed people to refinance their homes, take equity out and spend the newfound money to enhance their standards of living. While the mortgage debt of homeowners relative to their income is considerably higher than that in the past, low interest rates have reduced the debt servicing requirement. Moreover, the large gains in residential real estate values allow equity in homes to rise, despite sizeable debt financed extractions.

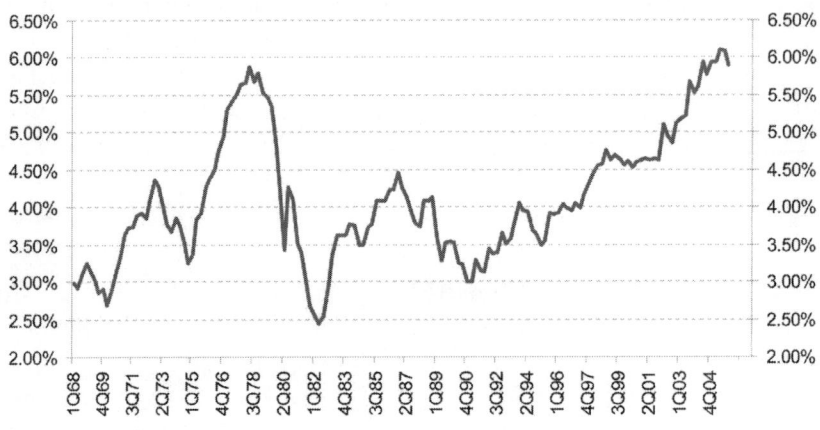

Source: U.S. Census Bureau and National Association of Realtors and Citigroup Investment Research – U.S. Equity Strategy

Increased levels of easy financing

The new, riskier forms of mortgage finance entice buyers into borrowing more than they normally would. A study by the NAR[62] indicates some important points:

1. In 2005, around 25% of all first-time buyers didn't need to make *any* down payment while buying a house and 38% made down payments of less than 5%. Some mortgage companies even offer buyers loans of 105% of the purchase price to value in order to cover buying costs. Home equity as a percentage of real estate value has fallen markedly in recent years despite rising home prices.
2. According to the NAR, sales of non-primary homes accounted for over one-third of overall sales. Around 23% of all home sales in 2004 were for investment purposes and 13% of sales were for second homes.[63] There are only so many homes that will be sold to speculators for investment and only a small percentage of households have the will and the means to own more than one home.
3. Payment option loans allow for the choice of several payment methods, including one consisting of payments that are less

than the interest due, which results in loan balances increasing as time goes on instead of decreasing, known as negative amortization. These loans work on the premise that housing prices are continuously rising and the buyer will therefore be in a position to sell the house at a premium or refinance it before any principal has to be repaid. However, because these loans are usually ARMs, the borrower is also exposed to the risk of higher interest rates. With the number of ARMs rising to corner a larger portion of new mortgages, especially in states experiencing the biggest price increases, regulators have rightfully begun to ask financial institutions questions about these types of loans.

Lax lending standards

Subprime loans now represent 10% of total outstanding mortgages. In an increasingly competitive environment, many conservative standards have fallen by the wayside. Lenders, appraisers and others in the booming real estate market have resorted to increasingly aggressive tactics to gain and maintain market share, including the following:

- Lowering credit scores required to qualify for certain loans,
- Increasing the debt that borrowers are allowed to carry,
- Making it easy for borrowers with little or no documentation of assets or income to get loans,
- Allowing customers with low credit ratings to take out home equity loans and lines of credit,
- Making it easy to take out interest-only mortgages, where only interest is paid in the early years, and
- Increasingly aggressive appraisals by some unscrupulous appraisers.

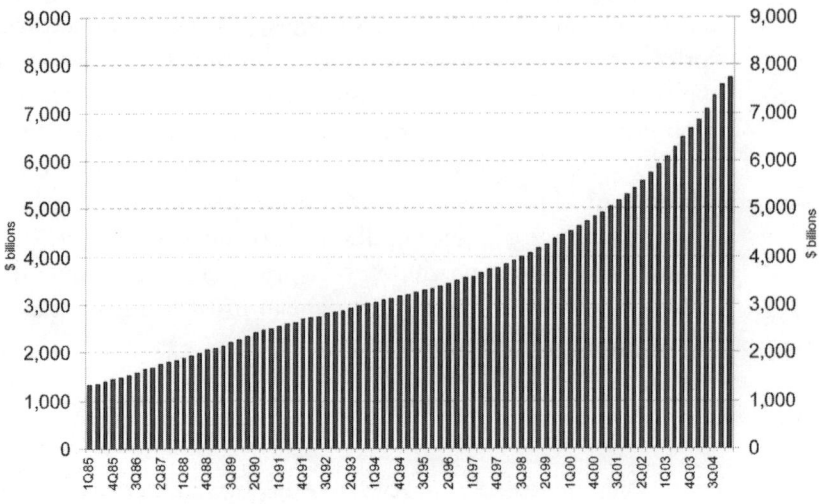

Note: Includes loans made under home equity lines of credit and loans secured by junior liens.
Source: Federal Reserve Flow of Funds and Citigroup Investment Research – U.S. Equity Strategy

Regional vs. National Prices

Housing price trends can vary from one region to another, but factors such as inexpensive and available credit have increased prices throughout the US. Large divergent trends between regions may not be sustainable, considering the average family spends about 30% of its monthly income on housing costs. So if home prices increase a great deal relative to the rest of the country, as they have on the West Coast, the increases would be difficult to sustain because wages would have to continue to rise there to pay for higher housing costs. Competitive labor market forces would take over, causing many companies to move work to lower labor cost locales.

It may also be difficult to isolate negative price trends to a particular region. Although the experience in past years would indicate housing downturns can be largely isolated, this time may be different. A severe decline in oil prices in the 1980s depressed the economy and housing prices in the energy producing region of the country, while prices remained buoyant elsewhere. However, in the 1980s the financial infrastructure for mortgage lending was local. The bank or savings and loan institution originated the loan and generally, unlike today, held the loan in its portfolio rather than securitizing it and selling it to investors.

Inter-state banking restrictions in place at the time further isolated regional specific problems to that particular region. Today, if a severe decline in prices occurs in an overheated region, rising defaults might impede money flows from national mortgage lenders and investors with exposure to that depressed region. The reduction in available liquidity for mortgage activity could result in spreading the negative price trend nationally.

Implications of a Bursting Housing Bubble on the US Economy

The current bubble is not only in housing prices but also in housing **finance**, and it has spread to other areas of the US and the global economy.[64] It appears to be a large bubble by historical standards, but having a better understanding of the dynamics a bubble exhibits, we have a fair idea of what to expect.

The bursting of the housing bubble would have a larger impact on the economy than the bursting of the stock market bubble. Housing is an asset that is far more evenly distributed among the population, whereas it is the wealthy who own a disproportionately large portion of the stock market. Additionally, housing real estate is collateral for over $8 trillion worth of mortgages and home equity debt, and although housing prices tend to vary less than stock prices, there is greater leverage associated with houses, so a lesser decline in prices would be required to wipe out an owner's equity. Also, the value of residential real estate loans and mortgage backed securities held by banks is substantially greater than the value of stocks held by banks. This can be important because losses related to the value of banks' assets will force them to reduce their lending activity, adding to an economic slowdown.

Direct impact of housing on economic activity

Housing is an important industry to the US economy in that it is a major source of income to builders, appraisers, lenders, real estate agents, glass makers, landscapers, roofers and lumber suppliers. Strong housing starts are also associated with higher sales of furniture and appliances, thereby stimulating the steel, copper, aluminum and plastics industries among others. It is estimated that the surge in housing accounted for 40% of the 4 million jobs created from 2003 to 2005. Since housing and related industries have driven economic growth in the past few years, any decline in housing could have a serious impact on the overall economy. The UCLA Anderson Forecast in December 2005[65] said that nine out of the previous 12 declines in residential housing were followed by recessions. From 2001 to mid 2005, consumption and residential investment together accounted for over 90% of the net increase in the GDP. Clearly, housing has been the prime job creator responsible for the economic recovery. If housing slows down, unemployment in this sector would rise. According to the *Forecast, at* least 500,000-800,000 jobs could be lost in housing and related industries.

Building homes does not raise the long-term economic growth potential the way building plants and equipment can. Plants and equipment are later used to produce income from the production and sale of goods and services with which to repay the associated debt and drive productivity. The debt generated in the acquisition of housing can therefore be described as 'unproductive'.

Housing impact on consumer spending

Research by the IMF indicated that from 1984 to 2000, in the US and similar economies, a $1 reduction in stock wealth translated into a 4 cent dip in household spending. However, a $1 reduction in housing wealth translated into a much higher 7 cent reduction in consumer spending.[66] With the current high leverage in the housing sector, many economists fear that any reduction in housing wealth will have an even greater impact.

The OCED, in a late 2004 study, suggested that housing wealth has a bigger effect on savings than financial wealth – people feel wealthier.[67] Federal Reserve data shows that homeowners' equity was only 55% in 2004, down from a sturdy 72% in 1986. But the belief they are getting wealthier through increasing housing prices, causes homeowners to feel less of a need to save. Less saving means more spending and this phenomenon was indicated by the high level of consumer spending over the past few years. Consumers have been treating their homes as sources of cash to upgrade their standard of living, not always realizing that home equity loans are in effect a means of turning over greater ownership of their homes to the bank in exchange for the loans. It is dangerous to equate increased equity to increased savings. Equity can erode as quickly as it was created.

Alan Greeenspan, drawing on new research, indicated that consumers have become enormously dependent on borrowing against their homes to fuel spending[68]. In 2004, borrowing against home values added $600 billion in consumer spending power – that's 7% of personal disposable income versus just 3% in 2000. The additional spending power primarily came in the form of net new borrowings on home purchases, cash out refinancing and home equity loans. $600 billion represents a truly staggering number when one considers that the total real GDP only increased about half as much in 2004.

Consumer spending represents 70% of our $11 trillion-per-year economy. If consumer spending – fueled in large part by home equity extraction and refinancing – has been the driver of economic growth, then a decline in home prices is likely to put the brakes on the rest of the economy as well. The CEPR report quoted earlier warned: "Every day, over 20,000 families buy a home, most at inflated numbers. The longer the bubble persists, the larger the impact will be."

While it is difficult to determine the potential cause and timing of a bubble collapse, a rise in interest rates (particularly the 10-year rate with respect to real estate) should be watched carefully. Bubbles tend to form when rates are falling and collapse when rates are rising. Lower rates have coaxed owners to draw equity out of their homes to spend on goods, services and investments. Households are spending and borrowing at an unusually high level. As indicated earlier, the household savings rate was negative in 2005 for the first time since the Great Depression. Household debt has increased from 65% of disposable income in the 1980s to over 126% in 2006. Record low savings and record high debts, along with excessively high asset values translate to a substantial risk of a downturn in the economy.

The nature of inflationary credit dictates that an ongoing accommodation of an expanding housing bubble will worsen imbalances.[69] The distorted marketplace is over-financing the mortgage finance bubble as the global environment of excess liquidity enlarges the global pool of speculative finance exacerbating imbalances. The confluence of vast speculative leveraging, derivative hedging and artificially low Treasury yields has broken down the pricing mechanism for mortgage finance.

In 2000 it was the stock market bubble; in 2006 it might very well be the real estate bubble. A contributory factor for both bubbles seems to lie with the Federal Reserve. While the Greenspan Fed had maintained that asset markets were not within their purview, the international view is that today's asset markets pose a great challenge to monetary policy. Central banks need to assess the risks of inflationary and deflationary price trends for asset values, not just the narrower basket of goods and services as measured by the CPI. Since the collapse of the equity bubble, the Fed has been trapped in a position where its monetary policy moves must be conducted in a methodical, slow and predictable manner (the quarter-point increases in the Fed funds rate every six weeks from June of 2004 up to July 2006). Any surprise move on the part of the Fed could have significant implications for the speculating community, housing and the economy at large.

Chapter 7

The Resolution of Economic Imbalances

A normally functioning free market economy depends on limited government interference and a sound currency. When government controls a fiat currency, both tenets are violated. A democratic government and a capitalistic economy provide an infrastructure that offers its citizens the greatest opportunity to attain wealth. Such a system has its own checks and balances. The root causes of the distortions in our economy are an unsound currency and the propensity for consumers and government to spend in excess of their means through the use of credit. If a sound money regime was in place, the amount of money available would be restricted by the amount of whatever was backing it, like gold. Increased demand for credit would be met with higher interest rates, discouraging much of the demand for new debt.

Alternatively, a fiat money system has virtually no restrictions as to how much can be produced by the Fed. Fiat money and an accommodative Fed allow for the expansion in the supply of credit to meet the demand for it. Forward thinking capitalists take advantage of the demand for credit in a system with virtually limitless funds and then over time a system evolves to accommodate the flows of funds. Commercial banks, insurance companies, hedge funds and others create and trade securities designed to link lenders and investors with those seeking funds. Evidence of the resulting credit bubble is found in inflated asset prices and narrow risk spreads. Ultimately, excess liquidity leads to imbalances, resulting in a painful reckoning for its victims.

It is natural for humans to aspire to affluence. Wealth means different things to different people. It can provide financial freedom and independence, social standing, enjoyment, power and the ability to help family, friends or others in need. When abundant credit is made available to the populace, many cannot resist the temptation to borrow and spend, attaining a false appearance or feeling of wealth. There is a big difference if one family decides to buy an SUV and has the earnings or savings to do so, while another family already struggling financially, gets approved for a loan to buy one. Each may feel wealthier and have a brand new SUV in the driveway, but the family that is struggling financially has a false sense of wealth and has only made its future financial picture more difficult.

From the time we are toddlers and throughout our lives, we are bombarded with hundreds of pitches each day from TV, radio, newspapers, magazines and the internet. Marketing has become a science as sophisticated campaigns and techniques are utilized to promote the purchase of goods and services. Retail space has grown at double the pace of population growth in the last 35 years. It is estimated there are 45-50,000 shopping centers in the US. We are surrounded by signs of excess. Excess consumption has become ingrained in our culture, but it would not have been possible without a denatured financial system.

Total household liabilities have doubled since 1998 to an astounding $12.7 trillion in 2006. Meanwhile, household debt rose to an unprecedented 126% of disposable income, versus less than 90% in 1998. The share of after-tax income obligated to the annual repayment of principal and interest, known as the debt service ratio, was 14.40% in 2006 according to the Federal Reserve. A broader measure of liabilities, called the financial obligations ratio[70], includes auto leases, rent, homeowners' insurance and property taxes. This measure indicated the share of after-tax income consumed by debt and debt-related obligations at over 19% in 2006. These numbers represent averages, so some people with low obligations ratios still have the capacity to continue spending. The growing ranks of those with higher ratios, however, have no choice but to cut spending. Both the debt service ratio and the financial obligation ratio reached record levels in 2006 despite reasonably low interest rates. The growing share of household income devoted to debt repayment leaves less for savings and other expenses. A growing number of people are finding themselves caught in a vicious debt trap, where more money must be borrowed to make ends meet. Unless real disposable income increases, consumers are close to or at a peak in debt service capacity, even if housing prices continue to climb.

A return to a sound economy requires a return to sound money. The best scenario would be for the government to act sooner than later. But drastic change is unrealistic in the absence of a crisis. Even in the aftermath of a crisis a return to a gold-backed currency is unlikely. Perhaps the best that can be hoped for is the situation Alan Greenspan described whereby the Fed acts as if a gold-backed currency was in place by restricting the creation of credit. The Fed could accomplish this in the current environment by raising the Fed Funds and discount rates to levels well above the inflation rate. Additionally, the Fed could conduct open market operations selling Treasury bonds they hold to drain money from the banking system. The Fed also has the power to raise the capital requirements for banks, which would reduce the amount of funds banks have available to lend. These are the tools the Fed has at its disposal to regain confidence that the dollar will maintain its purchasing power. However, thus far through most of 2006, the Fed has opted to continue to accommodate the demand for credit.

For the time being, foreigners are providing a large portion of the goods for Americans to consume and the money to purchase those goods. In exchange, the US is providing foreigners with IOUs and ownership stakes in our economy. We seem to be mortgaging our future, a state that Warren Buffett termed a "sharecropper society", where US citizens, whose country becomes owned by foreigners, pay a large portion of their production to foreign owners. An extrapolation of current trends would suggest such a result, but the likelihood is that these trends will reverse before we become "sharecroppers". Potentially, these trends can **change in an** orderly way if certain **behaviors and policies are changed**. Alternatively, the trends can change violently, resulting in monetary disorder and a loss of confidence in the financial system.

It is hoped that the imbalances in our economy will be resolved in an orderly way. Optimists point to the potential for cooperation between global economies, whereby each country makes adjustments to restore a more equitable trade condition. Exporting countries should stimulate their own economies to increase consumption, which would stimulate imports, helping to balance trade. If these countries are able to develop sufficient internal demand, their currencies would rise versus the dollar. A decline in the price of the dollar would further contribute to the balance of trade by making exports to them less expensive while making imports from them more expensive.

Due to the large trade surpluses with the US, foreign central banks have increased their dollar reserves at a rapid pace. Rather than converting the dollars they receive from their exports back into their domestic currency, they use their dollars to purchase US dollar-denominated securities. Foreign entities should reduce their purchases of US securities, which are done in part to maintain a higher dollar and instead diversify their holdings. Further, many of the net exporting countries could benefit the global economy, as well as their own, by lowering trade barriers and allowing additional imports. By stimulating internal demand, refraining from currency manipulation, allowing markets to set dollar exchange rates and reducing trade barriers, exporting countries could play a large part in normalizing global trade and capital flows.

The largest importing countries, especially the US, need to establish policies that discourage excess consumption and encourage greater savings. At the government level, eliminating budget deficits through increased taxes and/or reduced spending is desirable. The US's Treasury debt is enormous and the government should encourage budget surpluses rather than deficits in order to pay down principal. The urgency of budget surpluses and debt reduction is especially evident, considering we are about to enter an era where the 77-million strong baby boom generation will begin to retire, needing large sums of money from promised government programs rather than paying into them.[71] Although the issue of a balanced budget has been talked about for years, the lack of economic crises thus far has numbed the public into a state of apathy over the matter. Lacking a grass-roots demand for change, the heavy political inertia associated with the hard choices needed to balance budgets is difficult to overcome.

With respect to the consumer, if the Fed limited the supply of funds available to the banking system, interest rates would naturally rise if demand for credit increased. As alluded to earlier, such an action would help prevent a credit bubble from forming. In the absence of such restraints, other measures must be considered.

In early 2005, Greenspan advocated an overhaul of the tax system by combining elements of both income and consumption taxes to boost savings.[72] A shifting of the tax burden from income earners to consumers in the form of a consumption or national sales tax, replacing or reducing the income tax would incent an increase in savings and a decrease in spending. In our present system, once income is taxed, individuals have the choice to save or spend what remains. From a federal tax perspective, the individual is not penalized if he chooses to spend his money on goods and services. In fact, some forms of interest charged to consumers are tax deductible. On the other hand, if the individual chooses to save or invest his after-tax income, aside from limited investments in tax-advantaged retirement accounts, he is charged a tax for earned interest, dividends and capital gains.

A complete transition from the income tax to a consumption tax, although radical, might offer additional benefits. The IRS estimates the average time needed to complete and file a 1040 form is 13 hours for an individual. Around 130 million 1040s were filed in 2004. Collectively, the country could save 1.7 billion hours if the income tax code were abolished. Assuming the average individual's time is worth $20 per hour, this would translate to an annual savings of $34 billion. If the IRS was no longer needed, the government could eliminate almost $10 billion in annual IRS operating costs from the budget. Some private studies suggest overall savings would be much higher than those implied by the IRS estimates[73]. There are many things to consider when contemplating such major changes, but replacing the income tax should be examined.

Vulnerabilities

The credit bubble is vulnerable in a number of areas, any one of which could cause it to burst. The housing bubble evolved from Fed-induced easy credit in response to the economic downturn following the collapse of the tech bubble. The Fed succeeded in liquefying the economy as many people decided to take advantage of the inexpensive credit to buy new homes. Builders had difficulty keeping up with demand as housing prices soared. The 6% of the population who moved into new homes each year paid increasingly higher prices from 2000 to 2006.

Many, not wanting to move, were still able to take advantage of the increased value of their homes by extracting equity. The extraction of equity was promoted by a financial community that grew in size along with the demand for credit. Homeowners used the funds from the extraction of equity to spend on consumer goods and invest in financial markets. The direct impact of the boom in the housing construction industry, along with increased consumer spending, provided the elixir the Fed was hoping for. Foreign central banks and private investors bought many of the securities that were being created by the US financial industry. In the process, the demand for US dollar-denominated IOUs resulted in a stronger dollar and higher bond prices (lower interest rates). The artificially strong dollar and artificially low interest rates promoted further increases in housing prices, further equity extraction (loans) and further consumption. There are many areas of vulnerability in this chain of events which we will discuss next.

A decline in housing prices

One area of vulnerability is the risk that the prices of houses stop rising or even decline. This could be the result of several issues including the following:

1. An oversupply of homes in relation to the population: the percentage of households owning a home has risen to a record high from 65% to almost 70% in recent years. There is always a portion of the population that will not buy a home for a variety of reasons, only one of which is affordability. The increased penetration of home-ownership in the population leads to less potential future demand.
2. A fall in housing affordability if interest rates rise, impacting those with variable loans or those seeking new loans. Additionally, teaser rates on loans taken out in recent years will expire and rise to higher levels. Low margins for error for others who stretched to buy a more expensive home may cause them to struggle to keep up with higher payments.
3. A failure of income levels to keep pace with the cost of homeownership. The most common reasons for foreclosure are divorce, loss of employment or death, each event having obvious impacts on income. Wage pressures can also result from a traditional economic slowdown or a continuation of the trend towards offshore outsourcing. The proliferation of the internet and increased bandwidth at lower cost have reduced the cost of outsourcing. In recent years, higher-paid jobs requiring greater skills have migrated overseas. Now industries send work overseas to radiologists, lawyers, accountants, financial analysts, engineers and computer programmers among others. Wage compression in developed economies should continue, which can cause home affordability to deteriorate even if the cost of homeownership moderates.
4. A loss in confidence in the sustained rise in housing prices may cause speculators, and others who would have been tempted to purchase homes during the boom, to resist the temptation. A reduction in net purchases of homes from this group could impose a large negative impact on housing prices.
5. Lower income families that were financially in over their heads in buying a home to begin with could fall behind in payments and lose their homes. As lending standards declined, many people who could not afford to buy a home in past years based on their financial profiles, found lenders much more accommodating during the boom years. Many have no

margin of error and must make hard choices to cover everyday common expenses and keep up with mortgage payments. Some economists point to an economic plutocracy, claiming the impact of lower income families losing their homes and having to cut back consumption would have a minimal impact on the economy as a whole. Aside from the terrible human misery associated with financial hardship, the devastating consequences of debt default could very well impact the economy as a whole. Lower income families provide the housing demand for the socioeconomic level above them, allowing those families to move up to the next level, and so on. Generally, homeowners do not buy a new home unless they are confident they can sell their existing home. A disruption in this food chain may have ruinous repercussions for the economy.

A break in the long-term trend of rising prices for homes would result in a loss in the ability to fund future spending growth from this important asset class. Housing has provided the equity from which consumers could extract loans used to finance much of their spending. If housing prices stagnate or decline, equity extraction will cease to be a source of funds for a large part of the consumer base.

A short-circuit in the financial infrastructure

A breakdown in the financial machinery or infrastructure that evolved to accommodate the extension of large amounts of credit to home buyers and owners could occur. Financial companies have played a part at several points along the production line. Some companies specialize in the extension of loans to the consumer, others service the loans, others guarantee the loans, others package the loans, others create and trade derivatives based on the loans and yet others invest in the instruments derived from the loans. A breakdown in this production line could be initiated by:

1. Rising defaults and bankruptcies resulting from marginal buyers not being able to keep up with payments due to financial hardship or increasing payments. As financial institutions and investors with credit exposure experience higher default rates, their activities becomes less profitable

and in some cases, ruinous. Many leveraged financial entities have been aggressive in their approach to this market, so even a moderate rise in defaults can be devastating.
2. A mishap in the highly leveraged derivatives market, resulting in large losses of capital, could lead to avoidance of these instruments. Since some investors require interest rate risk or credit risk insurance, many participants would back away from mortgage debt entirely if these derivative instruments became suspect.
3. A hedge fund mishap, if it is severe enough, like derivatives, could result in a loss of confidence in the mortgage security market. A fund mishap could lead to an evaporation of liquidity, potentially imposing stress on the financial system. Again, this would disrupt the flow of funds, making financing homes at the consumer level much more difficult.
4. High interest rates, distortions in the yield curve or narrow spreads between mortgage-backed securities and Treasuries can negatively alter the potential for profits. If these circumstances occurred for prolonged periods of time, the result could be losses for financial firms, leading to risk avoidance and a loss in liquidity in the mortgage market.

In an environment where the finance mechanism breaks down, people might lack the ability to finance home purchases or tap existing home equity. This could lead to a reduction in housing prices and construction spending as well as a decline in general consumer spending serving to impair the economy.

A decline in foreign purchases of US securities

Foreigners reducing net purchases or initiating net sales of US financial instruments could create a shortfall in the supply of funds made available to the US. Due to a lack of savings in the US, this could prove to be more problematic for consumers than in past periods. Such a scenario could evolve due to the following:

1. Rapidly growing currency reserves held by foreign central banks due to high levels of net exports can lead to overinvestment and problems in their banking systems. As reserves grow, many countries try to "sterilize" currency market transactions in an

attempt to prevent inflation[74]. Sterilization refers to a central bank striving to maintain a lower domestic currency value in the face of capital inflows. The central bank often accomplishes this by selling domestic financial instruments it owns rather than the foreign currency it is receiving. This action serves to reduce the domestic component of the monetary base as the foreign component rises, thus keeping the overall money supply stable. However, it becomes increasingly difficult to sterilize inflows since continuous sales of domestic securities tend to raise domestic interest rates. Higher rates tend to attract even more capital inflows in the form of securities investments from overseas. This leads to an additional need to sterilize transactions.

2. A desire to diversify out of the dollar due to a lack in confidence in US assets or simply to balance foreign reserve holdings. If foreign investors decide they are not being adequately compensated for risk, or if there is an expectation of future declines in US bond markets (higher yields) or stock markets, they may embark on large-scale selling of these assets.

3. Even if confidence in US asset markets is maintained, the fear of a declining dollar destroying the relative value of those holdings can also lead to selling of dollar-denominated assets.

4. If the US adopted trade protection legislation, as many people in the US hope, retaliation through the sale of US financial instruments would be one of the few weapons available to many countries.

5. Other disagreements regarding political or military decisions by the US government could lead to retaliation by selling US assets, thus hurting it economically.

6. A rise in consumerism in foreign markets, creating a higher demand for money in their own countries would make less currency available for investment in the US.

If foreign investors sell or sufficiently reduce net new purchases of US dollar-denominated securities, the most likely result would be higher interest rates, a lower dollar, and lower US asset prices in general.

A breakdown in any of these links for one or more of the reasons cited could endanger the entire chain. The severity and rapidity of the resultant economic downturn would dictate counter measures taken by the US and foreign central banks and governments. As a general rule, the severity of a contraction in an economy approximates the magnitude of the previous expansion. Given that we have experienced an impressive economic expansion dating back to 1991, with the Fed successfully preventing any downturn of significance, we should not be too surprised if the next recession is much more severe than most.

If the imbalances discussed result in a recession, the intent on the part of the Bernanke Fed is quite predictable. It will act as promised in attempting to prevent deflation. But whether it could muster the force needed to counteract the powerful deflationary forces in place remains to be seen.

As opposed to inflation, deflation is a *reduction* in available money and credit, often accompanied by a *reduction* in the general level of prices. A decline in the real and nominal prices of housing would exert strong deflationary forces on the economy. If these forces become entrenched, they would be difficult to counteract. Without Fed or government intervention, the natural path for an over-liquefied, highly indebted economy experiencing a bursting bubble and slowing activity is a contraction of money and available credit.

The expanded ranks of marginal participants would be the first to repudiate their debts, leading to a contraction in the financial industry as losses mount. Those having to sell homes to satisfy debt tend to sell more aggressively at lower prices. Even those who did not need to sell would lose the thin sliver of equity they still had in their homes, leading to a negative wealth effect and impacting consumer spending and its 70% contribution to GDP. The newly unemployed would lack the means to keep up with mortgage payments, forcing many of them to join the growing ranks of forced home sellers.

The deflationary scenario might be likely if Fed intervention is lacking. However, Ben Bernanke has stated numerous times that if deflation became a threat, the Federal Reserve would move quickly and decisively to inflate the system through open market purchases of Treasury bonds, and if needed, agency bonds, mortgage-backed bonds, corporate bonds and even stocks[75]. It is possible that even if these measures take place, it may not be enough to instill enough confidence in consumers to resume their consumption binge.

Typically, a reflation attempt following a bursting bubble does not reflate the bubble, but manifests itself elsewhere. When the US reflated in 2000-2003, the tech bubble did not rise again. Instead, the excess liquidity was manifested in the US real estate market. The Japanese attempt to reflate its stock and real estate markets in 1990 by lowering interest rates to zero did not reflate those markets. Instead, much of the liquidity was borrowed by US financial entities, some of it in the form of carry trades. For example, a US hedge fund could sell short the yen and buy a variety of other financial assets around the world with the proceeds. As long as the yen was stable or declining, and Japanese interest rates stayed below the rates of others, profits could be earned and leveraged many times over. Thus the central bank's attempt to reflate the Japanese economy resulted in the inflation of financial assets outside of Japan.

In an extreme environment, if the Fed acted by buying every mortgage bond they possibly could, mortgage rates would decline to zero. But would that prompt many individuals to buy a bigger home? Probably, but if the potential buyers think it is very possible the values of their homes will decline, they might decide not to take out even free mortgage loans. Whether the economy moves towards deflation or inflation depends as much on consumer psychology as it does on monetary and government policy responses. The next recession will need to be watched closely for both – inflation and deflation – in order to determine the proper responses one should take.

A Fed that is aggressive enough might be successful in re-inflating the economy, but that too would come with consequences. Foreign **money would likely flee as the increasing supply of dollars diminishes** their value. From the US debtor perspective, the outstanding obligations to creditors would be diminished in real terms since bonds could be repurchased for pennies on the dollar using "monopoly money". But, it would become extremely difficult to issue new bonds. If the Fed was "successful" in inflating the economy, foreign bond investors would be the big losers, as would savers, along with those depending on fixed incomes.

Due to the fact the US housing bubble comprises such a large asset class ($20 trillion), it is hard to imagine what else could be inflated enough to revive the consumer. With our industrial base largely hollowed out, a bailout from capital investment is unlikely, at least immediately. Investment only represented 17% of GDP. So even a 5% drop in consumer spending would translate to a 3.5% drop in GDP. A 20% gain in investment would be needed to bring GDP back to even. Such a gain would be difficult given the large discrepancy between labor costs in the US versus other countries. However, if other countries have gained enough traction in internal consumer demand, then the lower dollar, and somewhat lower labor costs that would result in a recessionary environment, could lead to a potential bright spot in an otherwise bleak economy.

One area that might draw in newly produced dollars is the commodity sector. Although this might create an environment that would be conducive to speculative activity, the result of climbing commodity prices could have a negative impact on a consumption-based economy. Increased commodity prices would further strain already precarious family budgets as they did in the 1970s' "stagflation".

If confidence is lost in our currency and financial system, the creation of more currency will not be an effective salve. Gresham's Law dictates that bad money drives out good. People will decide to exchange their 'bad' dollars for things of value and substance which they will hoard. Commodities that can be stored, like oil and metals, might be bought even if actual consumption demand of those commodities is soft. The demand axis of the supply and demand curve typically reflects the demand to consume these items. But, if a monetary-induced demand to hoard commodities develops, the additive effect on demand could drive prices higher. As more dollars are produced, diminishing each unit's value, more will be required to purchase the hard assets, which renders higher prices. Commodity producers such as OPEC may decide in such an environment that they are better off withholding supply as the dollar declines, in order to receive a greater number of depreciated dollars per barrel later.

The Conundrum Explained

If the conundrum is how an economy can appear to function normally while maintaining staggering imbalances for a long period of time, the answer lies in the undeserved faith and confidence on the part of its participants. Economists examine monthly confidence statistics compiled in surveys to predict spending behavior. What the statistics do not reveal is whether or not having the confidence is misplaced or even destructive.

We have discussed various areas of concern in the economy that depend on confidence and faith – the faith a foreign investor has that the value of the dollar will be preserved while accepting a 4% annual rate of return. The faith a consumer has in his economic future that allows him to spend, running up large debts in order to enjoy "the good life" today while neglecting to save for the future. The faith on the part of government leaders and the financial community to not demand greater disclosure and standards from the hedge fund community and the derivatives market. The faith on the part of government that the housing GSEs can effectively manage large leveraged portfolios without undue risk to the financial system. The faith that a central bank possesses the ability to effectively dictate the supply and cost of the nation's credit and currency base better than a free market. The faith that a nation's currency does not require any intrinsic value or backing, that it will always maintain the value decreed by government. The faith homeowners have that the value of their homes will forever be maintained or increased. The faith of voters and the politicians they elect, that government can continue to spend money and make promises while putting off the method of payment for a later date.

Faith and confidence are the glue that holds our economic and financial systems together, but it is not strong enough to endure the stresses associated with our growing imbalances in the years to come unless dramatic change is forthcoming. We should recognize the dangers of continuing down this path and rectify these issues before they magnify the impact of the next recession. It is doubtful that we shall make the necessary changes in time. As a result, the next recession could be severe and prolonged and will most likely occur with an inflationary backdrop.

Regardless of how severe a recession we face, my faith lies in the **ingenuity and resiliency of the American people** to ultimately rebuild an economic structure with a strong foundation. We are descendents of people who were naturally optimistic, they had to be to take a chance and move to a foreign land, leaving behind friends and families, seeking a new start in a free country. They embraced the challenges of a free-enterprise system where those who work smart and hard are justly rewarded for their efforts. Our most competitive industries have always involved innovation and imagination; these are our trademarks. These traits are in our DNA, and we do not lose them when we face adversity. Indeed, history proves we are adept at confronting adversity. We are blessed with fertile land and an abundance of natural resources. We possess a powerful military to protect our interests. For good reason, we have been envied around the world, but our reputation for compassion and kindness has prevented envy from changing into hatred. We must combine these characteristics with a sound analytical approach towards our economic structure in order to chart a future path where we can lead the world to a future of prosperity.

Endnotes

[1] The website http://www.mises.org provides a large amount of content with archived articles relating to the Austrian School of Economics. The site is run by the Ludwig von Mises Institute.

[2] *Human Action: A Treatise on Economics,* Ludwig Von Mises, Yale University Press, 1949; 3rd edition, Regnery, 1966. pp 401

[3] Glyn Davies: *A History of Money from Ancient Times to the Present Day:* 3rd. ed. Cardiff University of Wales Press, 2002. pp 28

[4] Wray, L. R. (2000), *Modern money,* in: Smithin, J. (eds) *What is Money?*, London: Routledge International Studies in Money and Banking, p. 42.

[5] 58 Wray, L. R. (2000), *Modern money,* in: Smithin, J. (eds) *What is Money?*, London: Routledge International Studies in Money and Banking, pp. 43/44.

[6] In his thesis *Money Upside Down – A paradigm shift in economies and monetary theory?* pp 50, **Harald Haas** describes: "The tally stick was made of polished squared hazel-wood stick, with notches cut along one edge to signify denominations. The name of the debtor and transaction are written on two opposite sides of the stick. After contracting, the stick is split full length so each piece has a full record of notches bearing the amount of the debt and its unit of account for the contracted goods or services, the name of the debtor and the due date. The split is stopped about an inch from the base of the stick by

a crosscut, so that one of the pieces is shorter than the other." http://elib.suub.uni-bremen.de/publications/dissertations/E-Diss1237_Dis_Money_upside_down.pdf

7 *War Cycles/Peace Cycles – The Necessity of War in Modern Finance,* Lynchburg, Virginia Publishing Company, p 47.

8 *Money Upside Down – A paradigm shift in economies and monetary theory?* pp 58

9 *"Bad money drives out good money."* — Sir Thomas Gresham (1519?-1579) Scottish Banker

10 *Government Equity and Money: John Law's System in 1720 France* Frances R. Velde, Federal Reserve Bank of Chicago Nov 30 2003 pp12. http://www2.ku.edu/~econsem/Friday/papers(0506)/Velde%20wp2003-31.pdf pp12

11 From page 13 Page14: Doug Noland Credit Bubble Bulletin dated 8/13/04 p12-13 http://www.prudentbear.com/archive_comm_article.asp?category=Credit+Bubble+Bulletin&content_idx=35098 (October 03, 2006)

12 Warburg arrived in the US in 1902 and vigorously campaigned for a central bank in America that was modeled after European central banks. He was also the brother of Max Warburg who headed the Warburg banking consortium in Europe.

13 G. Edward Griffin, *The Creature from Jekyll Island a Second Look at the Federal Reserve (American Media, 1994, 1995, 1998, 2002)* This book provides a rich source of material regarding the history and role of the Federal Reserve.

[14] In 1912, the House Banking and Currency Committee examined the banking and finance industry and concluded that its control was vested in the hands of a few financial leaders, described by the committee's report as a 'money trust.' This was defined as: *an established and well defined identity and community of interest between a few leaders of finance... which has resulted in a vast and growing concentration of control of money and credit in the hands of a comparatively few men.*

[15] It was named so in deference to Senator Robert L. Owen of Oklahoma who had tabled a similar, companion bill in the Senate

[16] The 12 regional banks are based in Boston, New York, Philadelphia, Cleveland, Richmond, Atlanta, Chicago, St. Louis, Minneapolis, Kansas City, Dallas and San Francisco

[17] A series of speculative and other crisis faced by the pound made it an unstable currency, leading the US$ to become the dominant currency in world trade.

[18] Murray N. Rothbard: *The Mystery of Banking First Edition* (Richardson and Snyder, 1983) pp 146 http://www.mises.org/mysteryofbanking/mysteryofbanking.pdf

[19] http://www.tradedollarnut.com/Home%20Page/Home%20first%20links/Later%20Events/Late%20events.htm

[20] Between 1971 and 73, the Smithsonian Agreement pegged world currencies to the dollar rather than the gold in a fixed exchange rate. However, it failed to sustain the adjustable peg system with the new currency alignment and collapsed with the second devaluation of the dollar in 1973. Other world currencies were also left to float against the dollar. Later that year, the Basel Accord established the current floating exchange of currency rates that is the basis of the current international monetary system.

21 The Federal Reserve's funds rate is the rate banks charge each other for overnight funds. The discount rate is the rate the fed charges banks to borrow money from the Federal Reserve.

22 *Gold and Economic Freedom*, By Alan Greenspan, 1967

23 Gold and Economic Freedom, Alan Greenspan, 1966-67

24 Chairman Alan Greenspan Before the Economic Club of New York, New York City December 19, 2002 "Issues for Monetary Policy" http://www.federalreserve.gov/boarddocs/speeches/2002/20021219/

25 Ben S. Bernanke: *"Deflation: Making Sure 'It' Doesn't Happen Here"*. November 21, 2002 at National Economists Club in Washington, D.C.

26 Ben S. Bernanke: *"Deflation: Making Sure 'It' Doesn't Happen Here"*. November 21, 2002 at National Economists Club in Washington, D.C.

27 Ben S. Bernanke: *"Deflation: Making Sure 'It' Doesn't Happen Here"*. November 21, 2002 at National Economists Club in Washington, D.C.

28 Bernanke, Ben S, 1983. "**Non-monetary Effects of the Financial Crisis in Propagation of the Great Depression**," American Economic Review, American Economic Association, vol. 73(3), pages 257-76, June.

29 Ben S. Bernanke, Sandridge Lecture, Virginia Association of Economics, Richmond, VA. March 10, 2005

30 The Securities Industry and Financial Markets Association (SIFMA)

using the Bond Market Association's data. (Nov 5, 2003) http://www.bondmarkets.com/story.asp?id=84

[31] Testimony of Alan Greenspan before the Committee on Banking, Housing and Urban Affairs, US Senate (April 6, 2005) http://www.federalreserve.gov/BoardDocs/Testimony/2005/20050406/default.htm

[32] Congressional Budget Office, (Reducing the Deficit: Spending and Revenue Options, March 1997) http://www.cbo.gov/showdoc.cfm?index=6&sequence=17

[33] *Neither Fish nor Fowl: An Overview of the Big-Three Government-Sponsored Enterprises in the U.S. Housing Finance Markets*, Jay Cochran III, Catherine England, November 2001 http://www.mercatus.org/regulatorystudies/article.php/9.html

[34] Douglas Holtz-Eakin with Deborah Lucas and David Torregrosa letter to the Committee on Banking, Housing and Urban Affairs, (US Senate Updated Estimates of the Subsidies to the Housing GSEs April 8, 2004) http://www.cbo.gov/showdoc.cfm?index=5368&sequence=0

[35] OFHEO, (Report of the Special Examination of Fannie Mae, May 2006) http://www.ofheo.gov/media/pdf/FNMSPECIALEXAM.PDF Summary page.

[36] Federal Reserve Bank of Atlanta, Michael Padhi, senior economic analyst (Financial Update July-September 2001, *Bank Capital Exposure to Government-Sponsored-Enterprise Debt*)http://www.frbatlanta.org/invoke.cfm?objectid=5AC8E987-B0FE-11D5-898400508BB89A83&method=display

[37] Remarks by Alan Greenspan to the Conference on Housing and Mortgage Finance and the Macroeconomy, Federal Reserve Bank of Atlanta, May 19, 2005. http://www.federalreserve.gov/boardDocs/Speeches/2005/20050519/default.htm

[38] Bank for International Settlements, Monetary and Economic Department (*OTC derivatives market activity in the second half of 2005, May 2006*) http://www.bis.org/publ/otc_hy0605.pdf

[39] International Swaps and Derivatives Association, Inc (ISDA) survey released April 9, 2003 http://www.isda.org/statistics/surveynewsrelease030903v2.html

[40] Testimony of Alan Greenspan before the Committee on Banking and Financial Services, US House of Representatives July 24, 1998 (The Regulation of OTC Derivatives) http://www.federalreserve.gov/Boarddocs/testimony/1998/19980724.htm

[41] Berkshire Hathaway Chairman, Warren Buffett's Letter to Shareholders contained in 2005 Annual Report February 28, 2006 http://www.berkshirehathaway.com/letters/2005ltr.pdf pp10-11 This excerpt was reprinted from copyrighted material with permission of Warren Buffett.

[42] US Government Accountability Office, Fiscal Year 2005 Financial Report of the United States Government Secretary of the Treasury, John Snow http://www.gao.gov/financial/fy2005financialreport.html

[43] David M. Walker, Comptroller General of the United States, Current and Emerging Fiscal and Retirement Security Challenges January 14, 2005 http://www.gao.gov/cghome/cefrsc/cefrsc.pdf

44 Under long-range budget projections, the balances of the largest trust funds--those of the Social Security and Medicare programs--are estimated to gradually disappear, and the payments prescribed under the rules now used to determine the programs' benefits eventually would have to be delayed or curtailed because the programs' reserve spending authority (that is, the fund balances) would have been exhausted. The subsequent "unfunded" benefits arising through 2076 are estimated to be $16 trillion. This is the amount of benefits that could not be paid over the next 75 years from incoming receipts once the trust fund balances fell to zero. The figure consists of present value projections for an "open group" (which assumes new participants over time). The calculations are based on the 2002 reports of the trustees of the Old-Age, Survivors, and Disability Insurance and Medicare Trust Funds (figures provided by the Offices of the Actuary, Social Security Administration and Centers for Medicare and Medicaid Services). Those implied but unfunded commitments and such commitments of other trust fund programs are not included in the current summation of the government's debt. Source: CBO Release: **Long Range Fiscal Policy Brief No 3, August 2002**

45 Ceci Connolly and Mike Allen, Washington Post, (Medicare Drug Benefit May Cost $1.2 Trillion) February 9, 2005 http://www.washingtonpost.com/wp-dyn/articles/A9328-2005Feb8.html

46 Standard & Poors division of McGraw-Hill Companies press release dated November 27, 2006 (S&P 500 3rd Quarter Buybacks at $100 billion) http://www2.standardandpoors.com/servlet/Satellite?pagename=sp/Page/HomePg&r=1&l=EN&b=10

47 Reported under the Treasury International Capital (TIC) reporting system. Totals comprise both official and private holdings. (Data subject to revision). Source: Douglas R. Gillespie, www.prudentbear.com

48 http://www.federalreserve.gov/releases/Z1/20060309/z1.pdf Federal

Reserve statistical release March 9, 2006s Accounts of the United States)

[49] Federal Reserve Chairman Alan Greenspan testimony before the Committee on Banking, Housing and Urban Affairs, US Senate February, 16, 2005 http://www.federalreserve.gov/boarddocs/hh/2005/february/testimony.htm

[50] Federal Reserve Board Governor Ben S. Bernanke remarks to Sandridge Lecture, Virginia Association of Economics March 10, 2005 http://www.federalreserve.gov/boarddocs/speeches/2005/200503102/default.htm

[51] "The U.S. as a Net Debtor: The Sustainability of the U.S. External Imbalance" – Nouriel Roubini and Brad Setser, NYU, August 2004, revised November 2004. http://www.stern.nyu.edu/globalmacro/Roubini-Setser-US-External-Imbalances.pdf <accessed October 2006>

[52] Berkshire Hathaway Chairman, Warren Buffett's Letter to Shareholders contained in 2004 Annual Report February 28, 2005 http://www.berkshirehathaway.com/letters/2004ltr.pdf pp19-20 This excerpt was reprinted from copyrighted material with permission of Warren Buffett.

[53] Dean Baker and David Rosnik, November 2005, *Will a Bursting Bubble Trouble Bernanke?* (The Evidence for a Housing Bubble), Washington DC, Center for Economic and Political Research

[54] Office of Federal Housing Enterprise Oversight (OFHEO), September 1, 2005, *Largest U.S. House Price Increases in More Than 25 Years* (OFHEO House Price Index Shows Annual Rise of 13.4 Percent), Washington DC, http://www.ofheo.gov/media/pdf/2q05hpi.pdf

[55] Edward E. Learner, Tom Lieser and Christopher Thornberg, June 19, 2002, *In California, A tale of Two Regions as Recession Ends in the North, Expansion Continues in the Southland,* UCLA Anderson Forecast. http://www.uclaforecast.com/contents/archive/media_6_02_1.asp This publication presets a good discussion of the concept of valuing homes based on PE ratios.

[56] John V. Duca, September/October 2005 Southwest Economy, *Making Sense of Elevated Housing Prices,* Federal Reserve Bank of Dallas, using National Association of Realtors' (NAR) National Affordability Index http://www.dallasfed.org/research/swe/2005/swe0505b.html

[57] Cynthia Angell and Norman Williams, May 2, 2005, *U.S. Home Prices: Does Bust Always Follow Boom?* Federal Deposit Insurance Corporation (FDIC) http://www.fdic.gov/bank/analytical/fyi/2005/050205fyi.html <accessed 30 December 2005>

[58] Les Christie, November 18, 2005, *Homeowners with ARMs face big bill jump* (Many adjustable rates are coming due, and higher interest rates will add hundreds to monthly bills) http://money.cnn.com/2005/11/18/real_estate/financing/ARMs_coming_due/index.htmhttp://www.mbaa.org/

[59] Dean Baker and David Rosnik, November 2005, *Will a Bursting Bubble Trouble Bernanke?* (The Evidence for a Housing Bubble), Washington DC, Center for Economic and Political Research http://www.cepr.net/publications/housing_bubble_2005_11.pdf

[60] Department of Housing and Urban Development, Research Works June 2006, *Factors in Achieving and Retaining Homeownership,* http://www.huduser.org/periodicals/ResearchWorks?june_06/RW_vol13num6tl.html

61 Eleanore Laise, SmartMoney Magazine, April 1, 2004, Interview with Sir John Templeton, http://www.smartmoney.com

62 The Economist, June 16, 2005, *The Global Housing Boom, In Come the Waves* (The worldwide rise in house prices is the biggest bubble in history. Prepare for the economic pain when it pops), http://www.economist.com/finance/displayStory.cfm?story_id=4079027

63 National Association of Realtors (NAR), March 1, 2005, *Second-Home Market Surges, Bigger Than Shown in Earlier Studies,* Washington, http://www.realtor.org/press_room/news_releases/2005/seconghomemktsurges05.html

64 Doug Noland, June 25, 2004, *The Mortgage Finance Bubble,* Prudent Bear Credit Bubble Bulletin, http://www.prudenbear.com/archive_comm_article.asp?categoryCredit%2BBubble%2BBulletin&content_idx=33630 Doug Noland presents an excellent discussion on the housing finance bubble in this reference.

65 Chris Isidore, December 8, 2005, *There go 800,000 jobs out the door* (UCLA: Housing slump to hit building and finance employment, slow the economy, but no recession seen), New York, http://money.cnn.com/2005/12/08/news/economy/housing_bubble_jobs/

66 Alan Greenspan and James Kennedy, September 2005, *Estimates of Home Mortgage Originations, Repayments, and Debt on One to Four Family Residences,* Federal Reserve Board, Washington DC, http://www.federalreserve.gov/PUBS/feds/2005/200541/200541pap.pdf

67 Luiz de Mello, Per Mathis Kongsrud and Robert Price, July 13, 2004, *Saving Behavior and the Effectiveness of Fiscal Policy,* Organization for Economic Co-Operation and Development http://www.olis.oecd.org/olis/2004doc.

nsf/43bb6130e5e86e5fc12569fa005d004c/
620520f2a8ed2f3bc1256ed7007a844e/$FILE/JT00167451.DOC

[68] Alan Greenspan and James Kennedy, September 2005, *Estimates of Home Mortgage Originations, Repayments, and Debt on One to Four Family Residences,* Federal Reserve Board, Washington DC, http://www.federalreserve.gov/PUBS/feds/2005/200541/200541pap.pdf Greenspan's comments were taken from Greg Ip's article dated September 28, 2005 Wall Street Journal online (Federal Reserve Chairman Warns of Reliance on Housing Loans) http://www.realestatejournal.com/buysell/mortgages/20050928-ip.html

[69] Doug Noland, May 20, 2005, *Conundrums,* Prudent Bear Credit Bubble Bulletin, http://www.prudentbear.com/archive_comm_article.asp?category=Credit+Bubble+Bulletin&content_idx=43272

[70] Federal Reserve Board, Household Debt Service and Financial Obligations Ratios, October 12, 2006 http://www.federalreserve.gov/Releases/housedebt/

[71] Federal Reserve Board, Household Debt Service and Financial Obligations Ratios, October 12, 2006 http://www.federalreserve.gov/Releases/housedebt/

[72] Krysten Crawford, CNN/Money (Greenspan Backs Tax Revamp) March 4, 2005 http://money.cnn.com/2005/03/03/news/economy/tax_reform/index.htm?cnn=yes

[73] John S. Irons and Michael Powers, Center for American Progress, October 28, 2005 (Tax Complexity: By the Numbers) http://www.americanprogressaction.org/atf/cf/%7B65464111-BB20-4C7D-B1C9-0B033DD31B63%7D/TAXCOMPLEXITYREPORTTEXT.PDF

74 Jang-Yung Lee, International Monetary Fund, March 1997 (Sterilizing Capital Inflows) http://www.imf.org/EXTERNAL/PUBS/FT/ISSUES7/INDEX.HTM

75 Federal Reserve Board Governor Ben S. Bernanke Remarks before the National Economists Club, Washington DC November 21, 2002 http://federalreserve.gov/boardDocs/speeches/2002/20021121/default.htm

Made in the USA